COMPETITIVE SWIMMING

Techniques for Champions

Sports Illustrated Winner's Circle Books

BOOKS ON TEAM SPORTS

Baseball
Basketball
Football: Winning Defense
Football: Winning Offense
Hockey
Lacrosse
Pitching
Soccer
Volleyball

BOOKS ON INDIVIDUAL SPORTS

Bowling
Competitive Swimming
Figure Skating
Golf
Putting
Skiing
Tennis
Track: Championship Running
Track: The Field Events

SPECIAL BOOKS

Fly Fishing
Mountain Biking
Strength Training
Training with Weights

COMPETITIVE SWIMMING
Techniques for Champions

by Mark Schubert

Photography by Heinz Kluetmeier

Sports Illustrated
Winner's Circle Books,
New York

Every effort has been made in this book's preparation to stress the need for proper technique and safety when training (both on land and in the water) to swim competitively. Before beginning any swimming program, however, check with your health care practitioner to make sure it is appropriate for you to start such a program. Follow all instructions carefully, and be aware that using the equipment discussed in this book and/or swimming and diving could result in physical injury or even death, for which the author, photographers, Sports Illustrated Winner's Circle Books, and Time, Inc., will not be responsible.

Photo Credits: Robert S. Beck / Focus West, cover, p. 129. For *Sports Illustrated:* David Klutho, p. 12; Neil Leifer, p. 72; Paul Kennedy, pp. 146, 197; Steve Powell, p. 225. All other photographs by Heinz Kluetmeier.

FIRST SPORTS ILLUSTRATED BOOKS EDITION 1996
Sports Illustrated Competitive Swimming: Techniques for Champions was originally published by Time, Inc., in 1990.

Sports Illustrated Books
An imprint of Madison Books, Inc.
Lanham, MD 20706

Distributed by National Book Network

Designer: Kim Llewellyn

Library of Congress Cataloging-in-Publication Data

Schubert, Mark.
Sports illustrated competitive swimming: techniques for champions / by Mark Schubert; photography by Heinz Kluetmeier.
p.   cm.—(Sports illustrated winner's circle books)
1. Swimming. I. Kluetmeier, Heinz. II. Sports illustrated (Time, Inc.).
GV837.S355   1990   797.2'1–dc19   87–35445

ISBN 1–56800–068–5 (alk. paper)

Contents

COMPETITIVE SWIMMING
Techniques for Champions

Introduction

Swim racing, or competitive swimming, is an ancient sport. Records exist of swim races being conducted in numerous civilizations all over the world from all periods of antiquity.

Water itself has always been attractive to human beings. We live and walk near it, travel on it, watch it endlessly by lake or ocean, river, stream or pond. It's hardly surprising that we would choose to swim in water. We even build artificial ponds called swimming pools to have near our homes and schools.

By nature we seem to be a competitive species. As children we like to race, and we never seem to outgrow that racing desire. "Let's see who's faster!" is apparently a natural urge, one that only intensifies on the organized level. Worldwide, competitive swimming is the most popular participation sport, and in the United States, more Olympic gold medals have been won by swimmers than by all other athletes combined. For many years swimming has been our country's most productive Olympic sport, and swimming continues to grow at an explosive rate. In 1978 an estimated 260,000 American youngsters participated in competitive swimming. With the growth of Masters Swimming and large new programs for youth, by 1987 that number had risen to more than 500,000, with summer-only swimmers adding more than a million more young competitors.

Why such growth? To begin with, swimming lessons for youngsters are an American institution, and more and more kids are choosing to further their development as swimmers by joining swim teams. These teams may be sponsored by the local park district, by the YMCA, by United States Swimming Club teams, or by the local country club, but whatever the organization, the fact is that competitive swimming has become one of the most appealing sports in the United States for people of all ages. As well, in the past ten years, the

11

Top-quality competitive swimming programs are available nationwide to people of all ages and abilities.

If you're over 25, try competing at the Masters level. Many Masters swimmers find they perform better than they did when they were younger.

fastest growing segment has been Masters Swimming, competitive swimming for those over 25 years of age. The increasing exposure of swimming as one of the most health-enhancing sports of all is partially responsible for this surge in participation. Swimmers are healthy people with well-developed cardiovascular and muscular systems!

As you'll see, it's easy to become involved in some basic competitive swimming training. The purpose of this book is to provide you with some important information on biomechanics, the nuts and bolts of strokes, starts, and turns, as well as physiology, the rudiments of training for competitive swimming, and introductory information on dry-land training, workouts, nutrition, the role of mental preparation, and some thoughts on competition.

Whenever a book is written, there is a basic choice to be made that determines at what level the book will be useful. This book is aimed at competitive swimmers new to the sport, of whatever age. The concepts, plans, ideas, and instructions offered are geared for the novice swimmer, but it's hoped that the new, inexperienced swimming coach will also find much useful information here. The book is divided into eight chapters, starting with stroke mechanics (the most vital aspect of any swimming) and proceeding to the "enhancement" ideas of dry-land work and mental preparation. If only swimming improvement itself could be so neatly packaged! In fact, improvement is a combination of all the factors discussed here, and none is developed totally independently. As your strokes improve, you'll find that you gain endurance and strength, and thus gain confidence in your abilities—which, believe me, will reinforce your desire and capacity to learn new strokes and techniques. *There is no simple, linear procedure for improving as a swimmer.* Rather, improvement is a matter of working on a variety of skills in combinations tailored to your particular needs. To me, this complexity is part of the appeal of competitive swimming. It is a lifetime sport that can provide long-term satisfaction and reward. I hope this book will add to both.

—Mark Schubert
Austin, Texas

Proper stroke mechanics are a requisite to swimming well.

1

Stroke Mechanics

Stroke mechanics play the largest single role in creating a satisfying swimming career for swimmers of all ages. Learning to apply force in an effective, propulsive manner is a critical experience for age group, senior, or Masters athletes; and one of the first lessons you learn when discovering how to swim your best is that stroke mechanics can always be learned, relearned, or improved. If you haven't noticed already, you'll find that this constant refinement of technique to create ever-improving stroke mechanics is one of the most fascinating aspects of the sport.

This chapter is divided into several sections. The first deals with a method for learning the four competitive strokes: the freestyle, the backstroke, the butterfly, and the breaststroke; the next, with common principles that apply in all; and then four sections cover each stroke. Each stroke section is organized similarly:

1. Significant differences and similarities between this stroke and the other three.
2. A brief verbal outline of the stroke.
3. A detailed description of the arm stroke, recovery, body and head position, breathing, body movement, kick, and stroke rhythm.
4. Common stroke mistakes and necessary corrections.
5. A list of important drills for stroke development.

There is one additional matter to consider when you read this chapter. Those stroke techniques that we learn intellectually must be *put into practice* in order for improvement to result. The earlier in any swimming career that an athlete learns and employs proper technique, the more satisfying will be the progress of that career. This holds true for the newly initiated Masters competitor as well as the age group swimmer. It is never too soon to make stroke corrections and adjustments, and never too late. The more you practice your stroke technique perfectly, the better you'll swim and the more perfectly you'll compete. Conversely, practicing incorrect technique will result in a learning pattern that will take even longer to reverse than it took to form.

That being said, let me add that there is no one precise stroke technique that is "perfect" for everyone. Every person modifies his stroke technique somewhat, according to his body dimensions, strength, flexibility, and endurance. The important issue when analyzing your stroke, or when initially constructing it, is that it conform to the basic principles that have been proven by years of scientific analysis. Within this framework, the finishing touches you add to the stroke will reflect your individuality in the same way that the decorating touch reflects the individuality of the owner of a house. The key to intelligent stroke analysis and improvement will be your ability to recognize your mistakes and faults and modify your stroke. With this in mind, let's proceed to our first section, on the learning method for the four strokes.

THE VERBAL-PHYSICAL LEARNING METHOD

Most athletes use words to create pictures in their minds. This use of language seems universal, and is of critical importance in the teaching and learning of stroke mechanics in all four competitive swimming strokes. One of our tasks in the following sections on the strokes themselves is to create word pictures that will produce the image of the stroke that we wish to have as our framework.

To do this, we will begin our discussion of each stroke with a brief verbal outline of the stroke's components. As a swimmer or coach, you should use this outline to mentally view or review your own stroke. The purpose of these outlines is to reduce each stroke to certain key words or phrases that you can easily remember and review.

If you're a coach, you should use these key words or phrases in a variety of ways to "drill" your swimmers toward compete understanding of a stroke. If you're a swimmer, your ability to completely describe the stroke is critical because there appears to be a direct correlation between a swimmer's ability to describe a stroke and his or her ability to perform the stroke well. Swimmers who fail to verbalize correctly often also fail to swim correctly. Correcting your verbal understanding and description of a stroke can lead to correcting the physical skill by planting the correct word picture in your mind.

Initially you can improve your stroke ability by verbally reviewing the stroke with your coach or teammates, and following it up with dry-land stroke imitation drills. How do these work? Easy. You literally stand on deck and imitate the motions of the stroke while verbalizing the key words that describe those motions. Next, verbally review the stroke in sections and then wholly, without using physical gestures. Finally, get into the water and swim the stroke slowly, simultaneously reviewing the key words and phrases that describe it. Utilize the drills in each stroke section to isolate and "overlearn" the skills associated with each key word.

The goal is to learn the stroke so well that you can do it automatically. To do that, you create the proper word picture, then gradually increase the degree of automatic action while cutting down on the number of key phrases that you use as reminders while swimming. The skilled swimmer is one who has moved beyond thought-out strokes to a level of automatic flow. The beauty of this natural ease in the water is clearly seen in such artists of the swimming world as Mark Spitz and Tracy Caulkins. The most effective swimmers always appear to be moving with the greatest of ease. This grace in action comes from having mastered the mechanics of each stroke.

As you learn and master each stroke, the key word checklist becomes the perfect review device for use in warmup before competition. When stroke mechanics change, as they inevitably do during a swimming career (because of natural changes in buoyancy, strength, size, etc.), the key words become an important tool for you to reconstruct and repair your stroke.

Before we proceed to the specific strokes, let's look at the basic principles involved in swimming all of the competitive strokes. These principles of biomechanics are the keys upon which the verbal descriptions of each stroke are based.

COMMON PRINCIPLES THAT APPLY IN ALL FOUR COMPETITIVE STROKES

All four strokes have certain principles in common. The purpose of this section is to explore these common principles so that you'll understand the forces that affect competitive performance as they relate to stroke technique.

Improvement in stroke efficiency is tied to two general concepts: (1) *an increase in the propulsive force* and (2) *a decrease in the total resistance of the*

The faster you swim, the more you must work to minimize the water's resistance.

water to the body. Numerous factors contribute to these increases and decreases, and we will explore each shortly. First, however, it is important to grasp precisely how these two concepts interrelate, and the interrelation can best be summed up by the following: *The total amount of resistance increases by the square of the increase in speed.* Read that once again, slowly. Simply stated, it means that as speed increases, it becomes increasingly important to minimize resistance. The most skilled aquatic athletes, as we'll see, use a variety of techniques to minimize their total resistance during competitive swims.

Propulsion

In all strokes, propulsion is generated by the actions of the arms and legs. This propulsive force is a combination of the following factors:

1. the lift force,
2. the drag force,
3. the pitch of the hand,
4. effective use of a three-dimensional pull, and
5. the principle of acceleration.

The interaction of all these factors produces propulsion.

The Lift Force

In the skillful execution of any strokes, the lift force is probably the dominant means of propulsion. Lift is the same principle that acts upon the airplane wing, and is based on pressure differentials caused by the shape of the wing, or in this case, the shape of the arm and hand. In swimming, the hand and the forearm are "pulled" toward the curved surface of the wing (the back of the hand and arm), and lift is generated by the force of water passing over the wing. Effective use of the lift force depends on your ability to "scull" the hands across the largest possible number of water molecules. Sculling, which we'll discuss in greater detail later, involves contacting the most "still" water molecules possible with the hands and moving them a short distance, and it's characteristic of effective use of the lift principle. As we shall shortly see, lift is closely tied to the principles of acceleration and the three-dimensional pull, but for now, just keep in mind that *to generate effective lift force, you must scull your hands across the water.*

The Drag Force

"Drag force" is quite a descriptive term. A swimmer using the drag force literally grabs a handful of water molecules and "drags" them through the rest of the surrounding water. In contrast with lift, drag moves relatively few water molecules a long distance. *Drag* acts in concert with *lift* to produce *propulsion.* You needn't be as conscious of drag force as the other forces described here.

You will generate the drag force in each stroke *simply by following the prescribed stroke patterns.*

Hand Pitch

No matter the stroke, one of the most vital aspects of propulsion involves the pitch of the hand. What is "pitch"? Simply stated, it is the angle of attack that the leading edge of the hand has to the water. Just as with an airplane wing, there is a most advantageous angle that the hand has, relative to the swimmer's direction of travel. Hand pitch differs for each stroke and for each person, but several rules apply to all the strokes. In general, the thumb side of the hand should be leading the hand in its scull action, with the flow of water molecules at a 90-degree angle to the desired direction of propulsion. As you'll find if you experiment, *changing hand pitch will dramatically affect the propulsive effect of your stroke.* We'll discuss specific hand pitches for each stroke, but for now, keep in mind that hand pitch is a critical variable for good stroke mechanics.

Three-Dimensional Pull

All strokes have three distinct dimensions:

1. Length
2. Width
3. Depth

Effective strokes have changes in all three dimensions as the swimmer pulls through the complete motion. Interestingly, it's been found that ineffective strokes frequently *have no change in one of the above dimensions,* thus creating a "flat" stroke profile. One of the simplest ways to test your stroke effectiveness is to utilize a standard nonturbulent lane line as a marker. Note where your hand *enters* the water in relation to the lane line as you swim alongside it. If the hand *exits* the water ahead of where it went in, the stroke is effective. If it comes out behind the spot where it entered, it is ineffective. Next, note the three dimensions of the stroke. As the hand moves through the pull pattern, each dimension needs to change. For example, in freestyle the hand enters at the surface (shallow), then goes deep into the water, then pulls back up toward the body, then pushes back and deeper, then finally exits at the surface. At the same time, it enters at the shoulder line (wide). It also enters in front of the shoulder and pushes back, past the hip (well, actually the body moves past the hand, but no need to quibble). The point is that all three dimensions change simultaneously. In any stroke, if the hand is moving through a pattern of changes in each dimension, the pull is likely to be effective. If ineffective, check each dimension for change. Depth and width are two dimensions most usually neglected. Later, under specific stroke descriptions, we will detail the length, width, and depth dimensions that exist in each stroke pattern. For now, note that *all effective strokes have changes in three dimensions during the pull.*

Acceleration Principle

The degree of propulsion created by the lift and drag forces is limited by the amount of acceleration that the "wing" (limb) can manage through the flow of water. (Acceleration is produced by muscular contraction, which we will cover later.) As you will see, in all four strokes, acceleration of the limb (hand or foot) occurs from the outside toward the center line of the body in the beginning of the movement, and then proceeds, with a second burst, to the extreme extension of the limb (the closer the hand comes to the body, the faster it accelerates, then accelerates again to finish the stroke).

The final principle underlying all four strokes: *The degree of acceleration determines the total propulsion produced.*

Resistance

Of course, opposing the forces of propulsion produced as a swimmer swims are various types of resistance, three of which should concern the swimmer. They are:

1. Form resistance
2. Wave resistance
3. Frictional resistance

Form Resistance. Form resistance is the variety of resistance most critical to the swimming athlete, first because it is the type that the athlete has the most control over, and second, because it has the greatest effect on performance. "Form" means quite literally the shape of the body moving through the water. The bulkier the shape, the more form resistance is offered to the water molecules. The more streamlined the shape, the better for slipping forward through the water. This is true not only when considering the "still" shape of the body (a lean form moves more easily than a thick form), but also when observing the movement of the body during the stroke mechanics. Inefficient swimmers have bodies that "wiggle and squirm" through the water, while the effective swimmer always presents the smallest possible profile to the water through which he moves. Simply put, the less body the water has to resist, the easier the body will move through the water, which is why speedboats move more easily than tugboats, and why lean swimmers win more races than fat ones.

Streamlining affords the body the smallest profile relative to the flow of water. Later we will talk about streamlining in starts and turns as well as in the strokes.

Wave Resistance. Two kinds of waves affect the swimmer: surface waves and depth waves. Pools built for competitions are generally designed (1) to absorb the force effects of the waves generated outward by swimming bodies and (2) to dissipate those forces as the water returns from the outer walls. Gutter designs, nonturbulent lane lines, and other design features affect how "fast" a given pool will be for swimmers. Depth is also a factor, as shallow pools allow the wave that originates from the swimmer to rebound quickly and forcefully off the bottom and thus disrupt the swimmer's stroke and his ability to find "still water" to scull through. Given a choice, *competitive swimmers prefer to swim in the least turbulent water they can find.*

Frictional Resistance. Frictional resistance is simply the degree of adhesion created by two types of molecules rubbing against each other. The rougher the surface of one set of molecules, the greater the friction between the water molecules and that surface. In the case of swimmers, the greatest sources of frictional resistance are the swimmer's body and his or her swimsuit.

Modern swimsuits are made from materials such as Lycra that have a slick surface, reducing friction, and their fit is snug enough to be considered almost a second skin. Top swimmers sometimes choose a less slick suit for lesser competitions, in order to enhance the feel of least resistance in the slicker suit they save for major competitions. Similarly, both male and female athletes will shave their bodies before major competitions both to decrease the frictional resistance caused by body hair and to enhance their "feel" for the water. Most female and many male swimmers cut frictional resistance further by wearing racing caps. As you progress in competitive swimming, you, too, should consider these resistance variables; decreasing frictional resistance is an easy way to give yourself a competitive edge.

THE FREESTYLE STROKE

Presently, freestyle is the fastest of the four competitive strokes. This is because the stroke applies a relatively constant amount of propulsive force, and there are fewer dead spots in the stroke compared to the others. As you'll see, the arms work almost directly opposite each other and provide almost continuous pressure on the water. Over the years, swimmers and coaches have experimented with various body positions, and modern freestyle features a good deal of body roll to allow greater use of the back muscles and to increase streamlining. The kick, too, has been another experimental part of the stroke. Today swimmers use a variety of kicks successfully, from a "heavy," "driving," six beats a kick for sprinters (that is, six kicks per single stroke) to a light, balanced kick of two beats per stroke for some distance freestylers. Finding the right kick is very much a matter of personal experimentation, and more and more successful freestyle swimmers are developing the ability to utilize a different style of kick and stroke tempo in different situations. This is especially true in the international swimming community, where the ability to surprise with different tactics during a race can be of significant importance in winning. For example, over the course of an 800-meter freestyle, a swimmer might change his kick rhythm anywhere from two kicks per stroke to six kicks, depending upon his race strategy and position in the race at any given moment. Again, *every swimmer will modify the stroke to suit his own capacities,* but in general, certain guidelines always apply. For now, let's look at an outline of the stroke and then see how to develop each of its parts—the pull, the recovery, the kick, as well as body position and breathing—effectively.

THE FREESTYLE STROKE: VERBAL OUTLINE

What follows is a verbal outline of the stroke, which you can use to drill yourself in the stroke's key elements. Important terms and movements are in italics.

The Pull: The hand reaches out and *enters* the water along an imaginary line extending forward from between the shoulder and the head. The hand enters *index finger first,* with the palm of the *hand pitched slightly to the outside.* The hand *extends out* in front of the head *and goes deep.* Then *the elbow bends,* and *the hand sweeps back and up* to the *high point of the chest,* while the *elbow points at the side wall of the pool.* Keep a HIGH ELBOW! The *hand then sweeps under the body,* and *pushes through* until the *thumb passes the thigh.*

The Recovery: As you *thumb your thigh,* the *hand spins* and the *little finger exits* the water *first,* and the elbow lifts. The hand is *recovered close to the surface* of the water *and close to the body,* with *the elbow high.* The back of the hand leads the recovery to the front of the body, where the hand reenters the water.

The Kick is fast, fluid, and relaxed. The *kick begins high up* in the thigh and butt muscles, and continues down to *loose, flexible ankles.* The basic motion of the kick should feel like kicking off a loose shoe.

The Body Position is comfortably *high* in the water, with *good body roll* equally to each side. Body position can be adjusted by head position.

Breathing: The exhalation is done underwater in either a *steady* or an *explosive* manner. The head is turned as the hand exits the water, and the breath is taken in the wake of the bow wave created by the head. Inhaling every *third stroke* helps balance the overall stroke.

The Freestyle Stroke: Overview

Hand entry.
At the start of the freestyle stroke, your hand should enter the water index finger first, with the elbow high (A, B).

A

B

The hand enters the water on a line between your shoulder and your head (C).

C

A

The pull.

Once your hand enters the water, extend it out in front and deep (A). Note the outward pitch of the hand—about 45 degrees.

B

Throughout the actual pull, try to maintain a high elbow position, as shown here (B).

Point your elbow toward the side wall of the pool (C)

Push your hand back until the thumb passes the thigh (E). This completes the "pull" phase of the stroke.

as you sweep your hand under your body (D).

C

D

E

A

The Freestyle Stroke: Overview (Cont.)

The recovery.
The back of your hand should lead your arm's relaxed recovery.

B

Throughout the recovery, your hand should remain close to the body and close to the water.

Breathing.
As your hand exits the water at the start of the recovery, turn your head, which has been face down and exhaling underwater, and draw a breath in the wake of the wave it creates.

PROPER TECHNIQUE FOR THE FREESTYLE STROKE

In order to get your freestyle stroke underway, either dive into the water or position yourself at the shallow end of the pool, and with your arms extended in front of you, glide forward over the surface of the water on your stomach. As you let one arm trail backward, lift your other arm out of the water, bending your elbow and keeping it high, and rolling your shoulder on the lifting movement. Your arm is now ready to begin the first part of the freestyle stroke, the *pull.*

The Freestyle Pull

To start the freestyle pull, the hand enters the water at a moment when the arm is slightly less than fully extended. The hand's point of entry lies at the intersection of two imaginary lines running outward from the shoulder and the midline of the head. The entry of the hand and arm should be smooth and not cause undue turbulence of the water surface. The hand pitch on entry is critical. The first two fingers of the hand should lead the entry, with the palm of the hand pitched out from the midline of the body, at approximately a 45-degree angle to the vertical (see illustration). The hand then extends out and deep into the water, creating change in two dimensions, width and depth (width: the hand moves from the outside to the midline of the body; depth: the hand moves down from the surface of the water). At full extension the hand is flat, with the palm facing the bottom of the pool and slightly to the rear.

At this point you make what is known as the "catch" on the water: The hand and forearm act as the previously described "wing"; the elbow stabilizes in a high position relative to the hand, and the point of the elbow is aimed to the side of the pool. The hand sweeps back and UP, changing its depth, with the thumb pointing at the high part of the chest. This sweeping motion creates a significant surge of propulsion and acceleration: the "wing" has just found a great deal of water to flow through.

To complete the stroke, push your hand past your thigh, with your arm extending almost completely straight. As you move from the pull to the push phase, you should concentrate on accelerating your hand as much as possible. The little finger leads the hand out of the water and begins the recovery phase of the stroke.

The Freestyle Stroke: Side View

A

B

Hand entry and pull.
Starting the freestyle pull, your hand should enter the water with the arm somewhat less than fully extended. Note the hand's angle of attack, which avoids undue turbulence and starts the "catch" phase of the stroke.

As the hand moves back, out, and deep in the water, the elbow is high relative to it, and pointing toward the side wall of the pool. The thumb should be pointing toward the high part of the chest.

E

As the little finger leads the hand out of the water in the recovery phase of the stroke, the other hand has already initiated the next "catch."

C

As the hand sweeps back and up, changing its depth, you should feel a surge of forward propulsion.

D

To complete the stroke, push your hand past your thigh (some swimmers actually brush the thigh with their thumb).

The Freestyle Recovery

The word "recovery" has two meanings: the first and most common meaning is to "replace to a former position." This is certainly something we do in freestyle during the phase when the hand moves from the rear of the body to in front, in preparation for the next stroke. The second meaning is "to rest," and that, too, occurs during a successful freestyle recovery. The main muscles in freestyle include the various heads of the triceps above the elbow, in the rear of the upper arm. If you lift your elbow high, and in effect "lead" the recovery with this high elbow, your back muscles do the work and your triceps rest. If you push the hand forward in the recovery, the triceps work again, just as they do on the pull. It's vital, therefore, that you keep your fingertips close to the water and close to your body, and that your elbow stay high on the recovery. The action should be relaxed, easy, and smooth. The best way to see an effective recovery is to look at a good freestyle swimmer from head on. If her hand travels a straight course from thigh to entry, it is the shortest and most relaxed route. A wide or high hand position is the least effective. When working on a good recovery, concentrate on a high elbow position with the hand close to the water and close to the body.

A   B

The recovery.
Proper arm recovery always begins with a high elbow (A). The fingertips move forward, close to the water, with the elbow remaining high (B).

The Freestyle Kick

Regardless of the number of kicks per arm cycle, the mechanics of the kick are very much the same. You should kick with a relaxed but relatively straight leg, your ankles should remain flexible throughout the kicking motion, and your feet should be turned slightly inward. Good knee extension helps, and you should try to use your whole leg through every phase of the kick. Once you get the hang of kicking, you can vary kick tempo so that you'll be able to vary your overall swim tempo in specific competitive situations.

The kick.
In a good freestyle kick, the legs are relaxed but relatively straight and the ankles are flexible throughout the motion.

A

Freestyle Body Position

Body and head position during the freestyle are interrelated and critical, and you should pay attention to them at all times as you swim the stroke. Your head should ride at a point where the normal water level is somewhere between the eyebrows and the hairline. Head position affects body position in the freestyle. In general, the higher the head position, the higher the body position, assuming a good balancing kick. High body position is advantageous for sprinting but may be difficult to maintain for distance events.

As you develop your freestyle stroke, you should work on the side-to-side roll of your body for distance events. Rolling the body in a balanced fashion from side to side allows the powerful back muscles to help generate power and, in addition, helps reduce frictional resistance by reducing the amount of body surface in the water. This rolling motion can be compared to placing the body longitudinally on an axis and rotating an equal degree to each side.

Good knee extension helps improve propulsion.

B

Here the swimmer uses her whole leg through every phase of the kick.

C

Head position.
Your head should ride at a point where the normal water level is somewhere between the eyebrows and the hairline. In general, a high head position helps the body ride higher in the water.

Freestyle Breathing

The breathing motion during the freestyle stroke is quite simple. During the majority of the pull, your face is in the water and you slowly exhale your breath. Then, as your hand exits the water, turn your head along with your shoulder so that your mouth is in the trough of the bow wave created by your head. (In fact, your mouth is beneath the surface plane of the water, but in the trough.) Air will almost automatically enter the mouth and nose now, owing to the vacuum created in the lungs during exhalation. Your face now returns to its straight down position as your other hand enters the water for the next stroke.

The very best freestyle breathing is difficult to detect, as the best freestylers attempt to breathe with the least visible motion. As a freestyler, you can exhale in a variety of ways, using an explosive exhalation on the push of the stroke when sprinting or a steady, slower exhalation on longer swims. The critical key is to *work to exhale as fully as possible on every stroke.* You'll find that you won't

A   B

Freestyle breathing.
When breathing during the freestyle stroke, work to turn your head to the side (A), and try to hide the breath from view (B).

have to think about inhaling if you exhale fully, since the relative vacuum of the lungs will draw in the required air when you turn your head and "hide" it in the trough of the bow wave. You should take special care not to lift or "throw" your head on the breath, as this drastically affects body alignment and increases drag. Pretend that your head is pivoting on a spit running the length of the body, and keep the head on that axis when breathing.

Now go back and review the verbal outline of the stroke, starting on page 23, and try to visualize yourself performing each part of the stroke properly, as discussed on page 16.

THE FREESTYLE STROKE: COMMON FAULTS

The following are some of the stroke faults often made by new competitive freestyle swimmers. If you're guilty of any of them, rest assured that each is easily corrected with conscientious application of stroke drills. Needless to say, it's better to learn the stroke correctly in the first place and work diligently not to let stroke faults become ingrained habits, when they are much more difficult to uproot.

1. *Lifting the head when breathing.* Perhaps hoping to get more air, some swimmers lift their head when breathing during the freestyle stroke, which reduces their overall stroke efficiency. Instead of lifting the head, you should work to turn the head to the side and try to "hide" the breath from view.

2. *Neglecting to exhale underwater.* Often swimmers will neglect to exhale underwater, and find themselves trying to both exhale and inhale when they turn their head. The solution to the problem lies in concentrating on exhaling only when the face is in the water. Don't worry about inhaling. It should take care of itself. But if it doesn't, concentrate, as top swimmers do, on establishing a consistent breathing pattern. Again, breathing to a three-count, wherein you inhale on every third stroke, adds balance and rhythm to your stroke since you'll be breathing equally from both sides of your body.

3. *Improper recovery.* Some freestylers make the mistake of recovering with a straight arm. Their recovery hand may be high up in the air or out wide from the body, but both motions are inefficient in terms of replacing the hand in front of the shoulder for the next stroke. The shortest distance between the back part of the stroke and the entry is close to the body and close to the water. Lifting the hand high in the air or out wide from the body also leads to undesirable body motions that, in turn, increase resistance. A variety of drills for polishing your recovery are described in the next section.

4. *Improper pulling.* The most common stroke fault in freestyling is *pulling with a straight arm,* rather than using the pulling pattern described earlier. The elbow must bend so that the hand passes under the body in an elliptical pattern. This hand "sweep" is vitally important because it allows the hand to continually cut through new water molecules.

Nearly as common is the swimmer who pulls with a dropped elbow. This athlete allows his elbow to collapse from the "elbow-toward-the-side-wall" position and, in effect, leads the stroke with his elbow. By holding the elbow toward the side wall and concentrating on moving the *hand,* you can easily avoid this fault.

5. *Improper kicking.* A common fault in the kick action is to "bicycle" the legs, moving the knees toward the body. You can prevent "bicycling" by keeping your legs relatively straight during the kick and kicking from the buttocks down, not from the knees.

Almost as common is the kick that comes from the lower leg only, where the knees stay in the same relative position and the leg drive is in the calves only. The entire leg must act as a giant flexible fin during the kick action, not just the knees, calves, or ankles.

6. *Improper rhythm.* Any swimmer will eventually develop a natural

stroke rhythm of his own. Something to keep in mind as you work on your rhythm is that a constant application of force in the freestyle (or any other stroke) is preferable to a stop-and-go type of action. One goal of good rhythm, then, is not to let the pulling motions of each arm overlap, since that creates "dead spots" during the recovery. A good coach can help a great deal in developing a proper stroke rhythm for you.

Good freestyle technique can be drilled, so now let's look at some of the very best freestyle stroke drills, designed by one of the leading stroke coaches in the world, Walt Schluetter of the Mission Bay Aquatic Team.

FREESTYLE STROKE DRILLS

1. *Freestyle kicking on a kickboard.* This drill requires a Styrofoam kickboard to increase kicking resistance and to isolate the kick for development. Extend the kickboard from the body with straight arms, holding it with the hands only and letting your elbows trail in the water. Kicking workout sets are developed, just like swimming sets, at various paces and distances.

2. *Freestyle kicking without a board.* This exercise will enhance your ability to hold a high natural body position, and will help you work harder on your kick action. Keep your arms in front of you and breathe to the side.

3. *Freestyle pulling with buoy, tube, and paddles.* Pulling without kicking isolates the action of your arms and allows you to work on the proper mechanics of the pull. It also increases training stress on the arms. You can pull with any combination of the buoy, tube, and paddles. The buoy will help keep your legs up, on top of the water, and the tube is a resistance agent. The paddles offer an increased pulling surface and, thus, more training stress and an increased "feel" for the water. Experiment with different combinations of the devices to fine-tune the exercise to meet your needs.

4. *One-arm drills.* In this drill, you put one arm straight in front of the body, several inches below the surface, and pull with the other arm. This is a beautiful exercise for isolating the action of your arm in order to correct or to build stroke mechanics. Note: You can use this drill to work on both your pull and your recovery.

5. *Water-polo drill.* In this drill you keep your face out of the water, with your chin on the surface, and look straight ahead while stroking normally with both arms. It is an excellent exercise for developing good hand entries and for establishing a high body position. It also requires strong kicking.

Freestyle Drills

Freestyle kicking on a kickboard.
Grip the kickboard with your thumbs and index fingers grasping its upper surface.

Extend the kickboard in front of your body with straight arms, and let your elbows trail in the water. Work on keeping your legs relatively straight as you kick, and on kicking from the buttocks, not the knees.

Paddles.

To improve your freestyle stroke and increase the training stress on your arms, try using hand paddles (right) in combination with a set of leg floats and an ankle tube (below). The floats give your legs buoyancy; the tube restricts you from kicking.

6. *Dog paddle*. This drill is the age-old simple underwater arm stroke, with the elbows pointed out to the side wall. The strokes can be short, with the hands stopping near the chest, or long, with the hands pushing back past the hips. Keep your head above water or submerge it slightly. The dog paddle is an easy way to work on keeping your elbows high during the underwater pull.

7. *Catch-up drills with a dowel*. In this drill, one hand holds a pencil-size dowel and the other hand "catches up" with the first one and takes over the dowel, while the other hand pulls. This exercise can help you develop a strong kick and isolates the pulling power of each hand, while retaining the alternate arm action.

8. *"Chicken wing."* This drill is designed to enhance high elbow recovery during the freestyle stroke. To perform the chicken wing, tuck your hands into the armpits, extend an elbow up and forward, and try to pull with the upper arm. Follow through and extend the other elbow. Done properly, you should be able to extend each elbow forward and, in effect, swim with very short arms.

9. *Fist swimming*. One good way for you to enhance your feel of the water is to sometimes swim with your hand clenched in a fist, feeling where the hand is moving and working on a proper pull pattern. Alternate swimming lengths with a closed fist and an open hand.

10. *Thumb-your-side recovery*. As you finish the stroke, your thumb touches your side and continues to touch all the way up to the armpit. Thumbing your side in this fashion keeps the elbow high and helps develop body roll to each side. Once the hand reaches the armpit, either reach out to a conventional entry or slide the hand into the water for an underwater approach to the stroke.

THE BACKSTROKE

In the backstroke, perhaps more than in other strokes, proper learning depends on performing each part of the stroke properly. If you break the sequence of the stroke, there is no way to compensate for the break on the next step. Possibly this is because of the position of the swimmer's back during the stroke; lying as it does in the water limits the range of motion of various arm, neck, and leg joints. After all, humans were built to perform tasks in front of them, not behind them! All good backstrokers have learned to discipline their head and eye movements. The head must be absolutely still, and in order for that to happen, the eyes must be still also. All of us tend to move our heads toward where we look, so any eye movement results in fractional movement of the head. The eyes are also critical because through them we gauge how far away our recovering arms are from the surface of the water. If we move our head, we bring the recovery arm with it, and that results in an entry place that is too centered or too wide for an effective "catch" on the water. Each part of the stroke must be carefully constructed, and will be a direct result of the part preceding it. The need for such precision perhaps explains why at every level of competition, the backstroke has, throughout swimming history, been the stroke least "deep" in talent. Most swimmers fail to maintain the precision that results in success. If you are willing to study thoroughly and swim with precise mechanics, the backstroke might be your key to success!

THE BACKSTROKE: VERBAL OUTLINE

The Pull: The hand, arm extended, *enters the water* with the *little finger leading, just outside the line drawn directly out from the shoulder.* The first thing *the hand* does is *knife down deep* into the water. As the hand goes deep, *the body rotates onto that side* and *the hand sweeps wide and deep,* so that the *elbow is pointing at the bottom of the pool* and the fingers point to the side wall. At this point *the hand sweeps up and over,* and then *presses* quickly *toward the bottom.* Then the *hand sweeps up* from the deep position, and simultaneously sweeps across toward the hip from a position wide of the outer line. The hand exits near the hip, with the *thumb coming out* of the water *first.*

The Recovery: As the *hand comes out of the water, thumb first,* the *recovery shoulder lifts* and the hand is *recovered directly over the shoulder.* A straight line is formed by the shoulder, elbow, wrist, and fingers above the body. *The recovery shoulder* should be rolled inward and *lifted out of the water.* As it passes over the shoulder, the *hand is turned palm out,* so the *little finger is leading* into position for the entry. At this point the *hand drives down* to a precise, *smooth, clean entry,* with no splash.

The Kick is deeper than in freestyle, but *fast and powerful*, utilizing the whole leg.

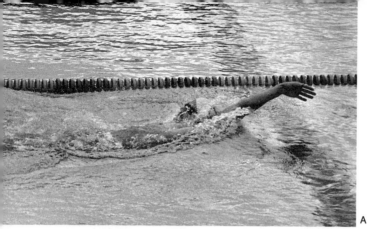

The Backstroke: Overview

Arm position.

When you perform the backstroke, your hand should enter the water little finger first, your arm fully extended (A). The hand enters the water on a line directly out from your shoulder (B). The wrist, elbow, and shoulder of the recovery arm should form a straight line (C).

A

B

C

Body Position: The backstroke is properly swum on the *side.* The least resistant position is *on the side,* so while *the head remains motionless,* the body has a *pronounced roll that lifts a significant part of the shoulder, back, and chest out of the water on each stroke,* thereby decreasing resistance. Low stroke count and high distance per stroke will lower the total resistance to be overcome in a race. *The head never moves,* and the eyes assist in keeping the head still *by not moving either.*

Breathing should be controlled by *inhaling on one arm stroke* and *exhaling on the next.* Rhythmic breathing is as important as in other strokes.

PROPER TECHNIQUE
FOR THE BACKSTROKE

The Backstroke Pull

Facing the edge of the pool at the shallow end, start by falling backward into a back float, and concentrate first on making your head very still. After that, lift your arm back straight so that your hand enters the water at a 90-degree angle to the surface, to enable it to proceed smoothly to a deep position. Try to make the entry with a minimum of water disturbance. Once your hand has gone in deep, sweep it wide, so that it "catches" the water in a position that is wide and deep from the body. (The body now has rolled onto the pulling side in such a way that an imaginary straight line running from the elbow to the shoulder joint of one arm could continue through the other shoulder and elbow. DO NOT get the elbow lined up "behind" the plane of the back, as this is a much weaker pulling position.) This catch position gives you a change in both the width and the depth dimension of the strike, enhancing its power and efficiency. Your elbow should now be pointing at the bottom of the pool, with the outside of the hand and fingers pointing to the side wall. Now sweep your hand toward the surface, then back down again, still fairly wide from the body. Pressing the palm down slightly, the arm remains wide and goes down deeper once again (another depth change). At this point, sweep your hand across the water and up to the hip, where it exits the water at high speed (width change and depth change). Always try to perform this last movement with tremendous acceleration.

The Backstroke Pull

 A

 B

 E

 F

Once your hand enters the water, it should go in deep and sweep wide to initiate the "catch" (A). Now sweep your hand toward the surface (B), then back down again deep (C), before accelerating it up to the hip (D), where it exits the water at high speed (E, F, G). The up-down-up arm movement is the essence of the backstroke pull.

C

D

G

The Backstroke Recovery

As your hand exits the water, it lifts the shoulder and recovers directly above that shoulder. Early in the recovery, your hand should be relaxed, and the back of the hand should "lead" the recovery of the arm. Keep your elbow straight, and raise the arm straight up above the shoulder, which is out of the water as your body rolls toward the other arm, which is now pulling. As your hand passes the 90-degree vertical position, rotate your palm to the outside and begin the recovery with the little finger leading. Your hand should then accelerate down to the entry, which is made just outside the shoulder line (frequently described in a clockface view, as occurring at either the one or the eleven o'clock position, with your head at the twelve o'clock position).

The backstroke recovery.
To initiate the recovery, the hand exits the water, lifting the shoulder with it (A). With the hand relaxed and the elbow straight, the hand leads the arm into the next stroke (B). As the arm passes the vertical position, the palm of the hand rotates outward in preparation for the next catch (C).

A

B

C

The Backstroke Kick

Other than being performed on the back and a bit deeper in the water, the backstroke kick is not very different from the freestyle kick. It perhaps provides a bit more propulsion when set deeply (that is, when the feet are deeper in the water than during the freestyle), and contributes much more than the freestyle kick to good body position. Always kick from the buttocks and upper thighs, and keep your ankles and feet very loose and relaxed, possibly imagining flicking a series of light beach balls off the toes.

The backstroke kick.
When kicking for the backstroke, keep your ankles and feet loose and relaxed; the power should originate from the buttocks and thighs. The kick is performed predominantly while you are on your side.

Backstroke Body Position

During a backstroke race it is vital to spend as much time as possible in the most streamlined and least resistant position—that is, on the side—and as little time as possible on the back, where the shoulders present a huge target for form resistance. Not only should you want to "ride high" on the water with a good kick and body roll, but you should also be concerned with the *total* amount of time spent in the highly resistant flat-on-the-back position. The number of times on the back is a direct result of the number of strokes you take. This suggests that the best backstrokers are those with a low total resistance—and a low stroke count! If we keep in mind that an increase in speed results in disproportionately high increase in resistance, then we can see that under the present rules for the stroke, good body position and low stroke count with high power will be the backstroke of the future.

Backstroke body position.
The key to swimming the backstroke fast lies in maintaining good body roll from stroke to stroke (A, B).

A

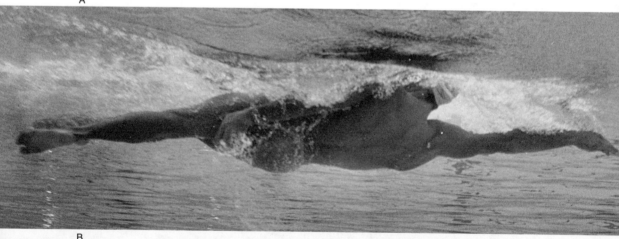

B

Backstroke Breathing

Since their face is out of the water at all times during the backstroke, swimmers tend to choose whatever breathing rhythm they wish while performing it. While this approach is not totally wrong, you'll improve the rhythm of your stroke by establishing a breathing pattern in coordination with your arms, just as you would for any of the other strokes. Exhaling and inhaling on specific pulling arms is the simple rhythm to establish, and you should take advantage of being able to inhale and exhale more fully than you can for the other strokes. Not only will you maintain better oxygen uptake by breathing this way, but also the slower, fuller breathing pattern may improve your overall rhythm in the stroke itself. Incidentally, maintaining a relaxed facial expression during the stroke increases breathing efficiency.

THE BACKSTROKE: COMMON FAULTS

1. *Improper body and head position.* One of the most common faults is the tendency of backstrokers to destroy the stroke by *moving their heads.* Whatever you do, try to maintain the strictest discipline in this area. Concentrate on not moving your eyes.

Backstrokers also make two other common body position faults: (1) *Swimming "flat" on the water.* To correct this fault, work toward a pronounced and evenly balanced body roll. (2) *"Sitting down"* in the water, which results in a very unstreamlined position, with high resistance. To avoid this problem, concentrate on stretching out and "swimming long" in the water. Some swimmers also *lean back too far* and are almost submerged in the water. In flat water conditions, strive to have water touching only to the lower portion of the ear.

2. *Improper pull.* Common stroke faults here include *swimming with straight arms,* rather than bending the elbows (sometimes only one arm is straight), and *failing to keep the elbow pointed toward the bottom of the pool.* In the latter case, strive instead for a "low elbow," which has the same beneficial effect as the traditional "high elbow" in freestyle.

Check also during the pull to make sure the hand is catching deep in the water. Many swimmers *rush the pull by starting to exert pressure as soon as the hand touches water.* Get the hand deep first. Again, remember that you want to develop a three-dimensional pull pattern, with changes in length, width, and depth.

3. *Improper recovery.* Frequently new swimmers will exhibit a bent elbow on the recovery. This hampers the arm's ability to relax while recovering and to line up its next entry properly. Get the arm straight and stretching up in a relaxed manner.

Many swimmers will either *cross the body* with the recovery arms or *recover wide of the body.* Both recoveries result in incorrect entry points. Be sure that your recovery arm is directly above the shoulder on the recovery.

4. *Improper kick.* The most common kick problem in the backstroke is a tendency to *bicycle the legs,* with the knees breaking the surface of the water. Bicycling results in an extremely weak and ineffective kick, and is usually combined with "sitting down" in the water. Instead of bicycling, try to keep your hips up, toward the water's surface, and "boil water" with your kick—that is, use a fast and powerful kicking motion which will result in much water movement at the surface, but keep your feet submerged during every phase of the kick. Remember, to aid propulsion, kick water, not air.

Next, let's look at some of the very best stroke drills to enhance the development of good backstroke technique.

BACKSTROKE DRILLS

1. *Kick on the back, hands overhead.* Kicking in this position is good for getting the hips up, and allows for faster kicking speed. Alternate this position with the other kicking positions described below, and be sure to do all backstroke kicking without a board.

2. *Kick on the back, hands at side.* Kicking in this position puts the hips and feet deeper in the water, and allows the shoulders to roll from side to side.

3. *Kick on the side, one arm overhead.* Since so much of the backstroke is actually swum on the side, this position most closely duplicates the actual kicking position of the stroke.

4. *Underwater backstroke.* In this drill you extend one hand overhead and
then execute a backstroke pull pattern with it while the other hand lies in the water next to the hip. As the hand pulls, the opposite shoulder rises out of the water. At the end of each stroke, "sneak" the hand forward, underwater, to the starting position. The key is to swim each length in as few strokes as possible. As you progress, you should take four, then three, then two strokes on each side. Eventually you will progress to recovering the arm over the top of the water. The purpose of this drill is to develop the most effective possible pull with each stroke.

5. *One-arm drill.* This is similar to the underwater backstroke, except that the whole stroke, including recovery, is taken with one arm. Again, its purpose is to isolate the one arm to help develop correct movement and an effective pull. The nonworking arm simply lies by the side, and the shoulder rotates with the stroke to facilitate the maximum shoulder roll.

6. *Head-still drill.* In this drill, you place a small flat stone on your forehead and try to keep it there while swimming and kicking, to enforce the principle of swimming with the head motionless.

7. *Double-recovery drill.* This drill reinforces the need to keep the recovery arm directly above the shoulder. As the working arm touches the water at the entry point, it reverses and travels backward to the hip, directly above the shoulder, with the arm straight and the palm facing out. Then it again recovers forward, enters, and pulls normally.

8. *Double-pull drill.* In this drill, both arms enter and complete the pulling movement at the same time. Pulling in this fashion helps establish a tremendous hand acceleration at the end of the stroke. It also prevents the body from rolling onto its side as it properly should, so the drill should be used sparingly, only to develop some hand acceleration at the end of the pull.

9. *Spin drill.* The purpose of this drill is to establish a rapid turnover—that is, a high number of strokes per lap. You should assume a very high head position, with the shoulders almost out of the water, and turn the arms over as rapidly as possible (spinning) without regard for pull pattern. Again, use sparingly, and only to establish arm speed.

10. *One-arm drill with the other arm extended into the air.* This drill helps develop the shoulder lift and back strength required to keep the recovery arm out of the water. Put one arm in a 90-degree recovery position above the shoulder. The other arm will pull continually underwater, while the chin stays close to the recovery shoulder. Strive to lift the recovery arm as high as possible from the water.

THE BUTTERFLY STROKE

Many people, swimmers and nonswimmers alike, feel that the butterfly is a difficult stroke to perform. This is not necessarily so, if you keep in mind the idea of using your *body* to swim the stroke, and not allow either your arms or your legs to dominate. The stroke *can* be difficult if you try to apply arm and leg force at the wrong moments. Rhythm and timing in the butterfly are of vital importance, as you'll see, and following the butterflyer's dictum "Hips go up as the hands go in" provides a simple and easy-to-follow timing mechanism that is foolproof for developing proper technique. When performed at the proper rhythm, the butterfly is a stroke of unsurpassed beauty and elegance. Properly developed stroke mechanics will allow you, even as a beginner, to experience the flowing feeling of a successful butterfly.

THE BUTTERFLY STROKE: VERBAL OUTLINE

Again, remember that properly swum, the butterfly is primarily *a body stroke.*

The body position, roughly similar to that of the freestyle stroke, is the basis of good butterfly action. The key to the stroke can be summed up in the line: *HIPS GO UP AS THE HANDS GO IN.* The body *rolls through* the water, with power added by proper application of propulsion from the arms and legs. The *chest* presses deep into the water when *the hips are on the surface,* and when *the shoulders and chest rise, the hips press down* to initiate the kick.

The pull is begun with the *hands entering the water together just above the shoulders,* the *hands pitched palm out.* As the hands enter, they *press* slightly *wide,* while the chest drives down between them, and the hips rise *(HANDS GO IN, HIPS GO UP).* The hands then *sweep under the throat,* with the *elbows pointing at the side wall.* The *hands almost touch,* then press back past the thighs and *sweep to the outside and up to the surface,* where they *exit* the water *little finger first,* with a rounding motion.

The recovery is performed with the *back of the hand leading* and the *arms relatively straight,* with *relaxed elbows.* The *little fingers are pitched up* on the recovery. The hands continue to the front where they reenter the water on a line above the shoulders.

Breathing is done with a *forceful exhalation on the push phase* of the arm stroke, and the *head and shoulders reach a natural high point* in the stroke *at the back of the pull.* The *inhalation is taken as the hands exit the water,* and

the *head is back down as the arms recover.* The head lifts up and faces straight
ahead.

The kick is done with both legs acting together as a big fin, and is timed to continue the natural body roll. The kick will fit naturally into the stroke when the hands go in and the butt goes up.

Timing is vital to a successful butterfly. *The body "rolls" forward, with the buttocks up and the chest down.* Then the arms exert power as the chest starts to come to a level position. *The arm stroke finishes as the breath is taken,* and the leg kick drives the body forward. The *arm recovery occurs* as the *chest goes forward and down* and the butt comes back to the surface.

PROPER TECHNIQUE FOR THE BUTTERFLY STROKE

The Butterfly Pull

In some regards, the pull is similar to that of the freestyle. Your hands enter the water on a line with the shoulders (stronger swimmers' hands enter closer to the midline, younger or weaker swimmers' enter wider than the shoulders). Entering "inside" requires a propulsive scull to the outside, which, in turn, requires additional strength. If you're not a strong swimmer, you'll experience greater success and remain developmentally sound by entering wider. As your hands enter the water, they should be pitched palm out, at a 45-degree angle to the water surface. Once they enter, they should press out slightly, while the chest goes down between the arms to its maximum depth or extension. Once the chest is as deep as it can reasonably go and your hips are as high as they can reasonably go, your hands, which were near the surface, should sweep down and in, toward the throat. Your elbows should be pointed toward the side walls in what is known as the "high elbow" position.

Once your hands come quite close together under the throat, they should press back and out, finishing with a rounding motion past your thighs. They then exit the water with the little finger leading. In this motion, your hands have moved from (1) the surface of the water to (2) deep in the water, to (3) a raised position under the throat, to (4) deep under the hips, to (5) the surface of the water at the exit. That's quite a series of depth changes! They have also gone through several width changes, from narrow to wide, to narrow to wide. Acceleration occurs as the hands move from the catch toward the midline of the body, and then again from the throat to the exit.

The Butterfly Stroke: Overview

A

B

C

The key to performing the butterfly stroke successfully is to remember: "The hips go up as the hands go in" (A). On entry into the water, the hands are pitched palm out (B). As the hands stroke back, they almost touch each other underneath the body (C). During the kick, in which the legs act together as a big fin, there can be considerable knee bend (D). On the recovery, the hands exit the water with the little fingers pointing upward (E). Just before the hands exit the water completely, the swimmer inhales (F).

D

E

F

A

B

The Butterfly Pull

In the pull, your hands enter the water with palms pitched out at a 45-degree angle (A). After they enter the water, press the hands out slightly (B). Next, start the backward sweep, down and in (C). Throughout the sweep, keep your elbows high (D). Press your hands out and back, with a rounding motion at the thighs (E).

C

D

E

The Butterfly Recovery

Arm recovery in the butterfly is done with a relatively wide and flat motion. Your elbow should bend slightly in a relaxed manner, and the back of your hands should lead the recovery forward with the little fingers tipped up. Keeping the little fingers tipped up is a useful method for keeping the front of the shoulder rolled down into the next stroke. In certain sprint events, some swimmers elect to "pull" the arms forward, but in most butterfly situations you should perform the recovery with a rhythmic flow of the body, letting your hands' exit provide momentum for recovery.

The butterfly recovery.
Once the hands have cleared the water, the arm recovery for the butterfly stroke is relatively wide and flat (A), with the head leading the hands back down into the water (B).

A

B

Breathing.
To breathe when performing the butterfly, extend your head forward, don't lift it.

Breathing

Breathing while doing the butterfly can be accomplished in either an explosive or a prolonged exhalation, depending on the distance of the swim and personal comfort and preference, but in either case, your head should be *extended,* not lifted, so that the chin is on the surface of the water, and the inhalation should be taken while the hands are finishing their underwater pull. During your arms' recovery, your head should drop again into the water, in line with the spine when the hands pass the shoulder on recovery. Always breathe with your head extended in front of you when doing the butterfly, not with your head to the side.

The butterfly kick.
The kick originates in the upper thighs (A). Visualize the kick as a giant fin action (B), with strong upward and downward components (C).

A

B

The Kick

In many cases, swimmers overemphasize the kick aspect of the stroke, and waste energy in an effort that is usually minimally rewarding. The mechanics of the kick are straightforward. The kick originates in the upper thighs, and then "flows" down the legs to the toes, where the final "snap" is through the ankles to the toes. The knees do bend, with a relaxed movement. You'll find that it's useful to visualize the kick as a giant fin action, requiring muscular action in both directions, kicking down and then back up. To the advanced competitor, the speed of the hips is of particular importance, since keeping a sharp, quick hip action at the end of a race helps determine and accelerate stroke tempo.

THE BUTTERFLY STROKE: COMMON FAULTS

1. *Improper body position.* Many swimmers attempt to swim the butterfly (or the "fly," as it's called) with a *flat body position.* The body must roll forward in the water for effective butterfly action. Think of your body "sliding" forward from the hips to the chest in the hand entry phase. A flat rigid body makes for a weak, ineffective kick and, in effect, forces the arms to do most of the propulsive work.

c

2. *Improper pull pattern.* Another common error is to *fail to get the hands in under the throat.* The swimmer will pull down the outline of the body instead of getting underneath the body. Other swimmers *allow the hands to enter too close to the centerline of the body.* This requires a great deal of strength and robs energy necessary for completing a race. Still, every swimmer's strength and body composition are different. The best way to determine the proper entry position for your arms is to experiment.

3. *Improper kick.* Often swimmers just learning the fly *will try to kick too hard,* resulting in very poor timing. When learning the butterfly, let your kick *just fit* into the body motion; you can accentuate the kick action later in your stroke development.

4. *Improper arm recovery.* Some swimmers try to bring the hands out of the water *with the thumb leading.* The result is an awkward recovery. Always remember that for the rest of the stroke to be able to fall into place, the little finger must exit the water first.

Another recovery fault is trying to lift the elbows, creating *a high elbow recovery.* This results in the body "climbing" out of the water and makes the next pull extremely difficult. Remember, contrary to what the name suggests, the "fly" is swum *in* the water, not over it.

5. *Improper breathing.* Swimmers frequently attempt to inhale at the wrong spot in the stroke. They may try *too early,* when the hands are still in the powerful under-the-body phase, or *too late,* when the arms are trying to recover over the water. On occasion, one will see a swimmer trying to *breathe to the side.* All these breathing techniques are wrong. You must take your breath at the back of the pull, neither too early nor too late, and never from the side.

Okay, let's look at a series of excellent stroke drills for the butterfly.

BUTTERFLY STROKE DRILLS

1. *Kick on a board.* This is a standard drill for all strokes. Concentrate on forcing the front of the board down as you kick, so your hips come up.

2. *Kick on your side, lower hand extended underwater, so that there is water pressure on both sides of your legs.* A great drill for increasing the feel of the water on your feet.

3. *Kick on your back.* This drill, when performed with the fly kick, will remind you to kick in both directions, both up and down, and will teach you that the muscles required for kicking in each direction are much different. Both need development.

4. *One-arm fly.* This is the most useful fly drill going. In it, you swim with one arm only, while the other either extends in front of you or trails to the rear. Concentrate on timing, getting the hips to go up as the hand enters. You can do this drill for long distances to establish stroke rhythm and tempo. It is also useful for working on the arm recovery position. In either case, breathe to the front.

5. *Left arm, right arm, both arms.* A variation of the one-arm fly, you can swim with each arm taking one stroke, then add a full stroke, with both arms pulling together, as in regular fly. The trick is to stick to the rhythm of "hand goes in, hips go up." You can also go two left, two right, and then two double, and all sorts of variations of that pattern.

6. *Triple-kick fly.* Simply use three kicks between arm strokes, rather than two. This allows the arms extra rest, and can help young swimmers in establishing a rhythm. Useful in limited measure for older swimmers too.

7. *Fly with head up.* This is a strengthening exercise, much like the waterpolo freestyle drill (page 35), that will really build the leg kick necessary to keep the head out of the water during the arm recovery.

8. *Slide drill.* In this drill, you allow the hands to enter the water, then concentrate on letting the chest slide forward in the water while holding a two count before you pull. To do this properly, you must have your hips up high during the hand entry, so that the momentum you gain can "flow through" the shoulders.

9. *Push-off drill.* If you are new to the butterfly stroke, one good way to learn the body motion is to work in shallow water (3 to 4 feet deep), diving to the bottom and pushing off of it with your hands, then letting the hips break the surface while you get a breath, then diving down again to push off with the hands. This fun drill gets you moving like a dolphin and accentuates your need for body involvement in the stroke.

10. *Recovery drills.* While doing a one-arm butterfly, practice recovering in two ways: first, by pulling the arms forward, using the shoulder muscles; and second, by allowing the arms to recover with the flow of the body motion, known in competitive swimming as ballistic recovery.

THE BREASTSTROKE

The rules for swimming the breaststroke are undergoing some scrutiny right now, and some radical changes were made in 1986 to allow the head to go underwater as long as it surfaced once each stroke cycle. This has allowed for much increased body roll and body movement to the stroke, improving the potential for increased speed.

The breaststroke has always been the slowest of the competitive strokes, and speed is very dependent on the swimmer's ability to produce high power levels, relative to weight and body shape. These variables have also produced a greater-than-usual variation of opinion as to the proper mechanics for this stroke. Indeed, many different styles of breaststroke have been successful throughout its history.

THE BREASTSTROKE: VERBAL OUTLINE

The arm pull in the breaststroke is begun with the *hands stretching out and deep* in front of the body. The *hands are pitched out,* palms toward the pool walls, the index fingers together and the thumbs pointing down. The *elbows are straight.* The hands *press wide and pitch* the little finger up as they sweep out. When the *hands are wider than the shoulders,* the elbows stay up, and the *hands sweep deep and inward,* with the thumbs leading. As the *hands pass under the elbows,* the forearms are vertical, and the *elbows then squeeze together* under the chin.

The recovery is performed by keeping the hands and elbows close together

The Breaststroke: Overview

At the start of the breaststroke, the hands are stretched out and deep in front of the body (A). The elbows are straight (B), the hands are pitched out, palms toward the pool walls,

A

B

and "kicking" the hands forward, while the legs kick. This is done in the most streamlined manner possible.

The kick is begun with the *heels set up just outside the hips,* with the *toes turned outward* as far as possible. The feet and *legs kick wide, squeeze, extend,* and lift, then recover quickly outside the butt and hips.

Body position is *relatively flat* during the breaststroke, on the surface of the water. Some swimmers incorporate a certain amount of *body roll* into the rhythm of the stroke.

Breathing is done with the head held still, at the *natural high point* of the stroke as the body lifts at the end of the pull.

The mechanics of how and when to breathe during the breaststroke are relatively simple. The body will lift naturally as the elbows squeeze under the chin prior to and during the recovery. The inhalation is taken at this high point, with a minimum of head motion. As with the other strokes, the exhalation is done underwater. The swimmer breathes on every stroke. There is no advantage in skipping a breath, because the body will lift high enough to breathe anyway. In fact, it's foolish to miss this opportunity for air.

Stroke rhythm is vital to good breaststroke. Generally, try to envision a "kick, stretch, pull" sequence, with some overlap between the kick and pull at faster speeds. When kicking, the arms must be streamlined; when pulling, the legs must be streamlined.

thumbs pointing downward (C). As the pull begins, the hands press wide, with the little finger pitching up (D). As soon as they have moved wider than the shoulders, the hands sweep

(continued on next page)

C

D

The Breaststroke: Overview (Cont.)

E

F

I

J

deep and inward, with the elbows remaining up (E). As the hands pass under the elbows, the forearms are vertical (F). On the recovery, the elbows squeeze together under the chin (G), and the hands and elbows stay close together (H). Then the kick begins, with the heels just outside the plane of the hips, the toes turned outward as far as possible, and the knees closer together than the feet (I). The feet and legs kick wide (J), squeeze (K), extend, lift, and the next stroke begins.

G

H

K

PROPER TECHNIQUE FOR THE BREASTSTROKE

The Breaststroke Pull

Begin the breaststroke pull with your hands extended from the front of your body and 8 to 12 inches below the surface of the water. Your index fingers should be together, and your thumbs together and pointing down, putting the palms of your hands at roughly a 45-degree angle to the vertical. Your first action is an outward press of the hand that extends considerably wider than the shoulders, but varies by individual. At the end of the outward press, your hands should be vertical in the water, with the little finger pitched up, toward the surface. The next motion is a downward and inward sweep of the hands, changing both width and depth of the stroke. As your forearm sweeps in, hold it as close to vertical in the water as possible, with the elbow holding high and still. As your hands pass under your elbows, the elbows and upper arms follow your hands inward and squeeze under the chin. Your hands then accelerate from the outside to the inside. During the pull, depth dimensions and width change should be obvious. Less obvious is the change in the length dimension, but the hands should finish considerably forward of where they began their outward sweep. If you examine the technique closely, you'll see that there are clear applications of the sculling principle in the breaststroke pull.

The Breaststroke Kick

Begin the kick with your heels drawn up outside your hips, as "high" as possible. Your knees remain extended from the body. Kick your legs wide, with your toes turned out maximally, and then kick back, around, and deep. As your feet come together at the back part of the kick, squeeze your legs all the way up, so that your thighs come together, and then lift your feet and lower legs toward the surface. This later movement helps effect a smooth, quick leg recovery.

The Breaststroke Pull

The breaststroke pull begins with your hands in front of you and slightly below the water's surface (A). Press your hands outward, wide, beyond the plane of the shoulders. At the end of the outward press, your thumbs should be down and your hands vertical (B). As you sweep your forearms in to complete the stroke, hold the elbows high (C, D).

A

B

C

D

The Breaststroke Kick

A

B

E

F

C

D

Begin the kick by bringing your heels up high, near the buttocks, and separating your knees (A, B). Now kick your legs out wide with your toes turned outward as far as possible (C), and then kick back in an arc, keeping the legs deep (D). As your feet come together, so should your legs (E). Now lift your feet and lower legs toward the water's surface (F) in preparation for the next stroke.

Body Position

You can either hold your body flat, or you can roll the stroke by lifting your hips closer to the surface as your hands extend in front, then lifting your upper body as the hands finish and begin to recover. This roll has the advantage of lifting the shoulders and chest out of the water as the force of the kick drives the rest of the body forward. It then gets the hips up and streamlined while the arms begin to apply force.

The breaststroke: body position.
Throughout the breaststroke your body position should be relatively flat and streamlined, with a slight rolling or undulating motion from stroke to stroke.

1. *Faulty rhythm.* Oftentimes, novice swimmers will try to kick and pull at the same time. To avoid this fault, try to kick first, then stretch, then pull. *Separate* the propulsive actions.

2. *Improper kick.* Novice swimmers will also frequently kick straight back rather than rounding the kick. This time, think of the length, width, and depth changes in all phases of the stroke. A rounded kick will necessarily follow.

Too, novice swimmers will fail to get the toes turned out, which greatly reduces the sculling potential of the feet. This makes it difficult to "hold the water" with the legs. Turn the toes out, so that your feet and legs can provide propulsive force. Also try to avoid incomplete leg recovery—another common fault—as this, in effect, creates a weak half-kick.

3. *Improper pull.* Some swimmers will fail to pull wide enough. Solution: Make your hands perform their outward press outside the plane of the shoulders.

Other common pulling faults: *Pressing too wide.* Result: a weak arm stroke. Experiment to find the proper width.

Failing to keep the elbows up. The swimmer tries to pull the whole arm into the midline at once. Remember, hands move across first.

Failure to turn the fingers down. At the end of the pull, the forearms must be vertical in the water.

4. *Improper recovery.* Swimmers who fail to keep their hands together at the start of the recovery create much higher resistance levels with their hands and arms than necessary. Keep those hands together. Too, be sure not to begin your next pull too early lest you lose the propulsive value of your kick.

5. *Breathing.* It's common to see swimmers breathing either too late or much too soon. To curb this fault, swim with your face in the water for a bit to discover the naturally highest point of the stroke. That high point is when you should inhale. Finally, don't try to inhale *and* exhale during the head lift—exhale underwater—and always try to breathe with as little head motion as possible.

Now let's look at some drills to develop your breaststroke.

1. *Kick on a board.* Hold the board as you would for a freestyle kicking drill, but do a breaststroke kick instead. As you'll quickly discover, the board allows for slow, purposeful kick mechanics.

2. *Kick with hands in back.* Place the hands near the hips, with the fingertips trailing in the water. Bring the heels up and touch the fingers with the heels. This drill ensures that the feet recover all the way up to the hips before they begin to kick.

3. *Kick with hands in front.* In this drill, you lock your hands together in front of the body, and keep the elbows locked while you kick the body forward. This is the best kicking drill for developing hip lift for a "rolling" breaststroke style. It is also most similar to the kicking style used in the actual stroke.

4. *Kick on the back.* Breaststroke kicking while on the back is an excellent method for concentrating on keeping the hips and the knees lined up in the same vertical plane. Simply turn over onto your back, and execute the same breaststroke kick! It is impossible to do this incorrectly, as long as you keep your knees in the water.

5. *Two kicks and a pull.* This drill is used for both sharpening one's timing and strengthening one's kick. The rhythm is: kick, kick and stretch, pull. Done properly, it helps you learn to "ride" the kick before beginning your pull.

6. *Kick-stretch-pull.* A modification of the drill above, this one allows a pause between the kick and the pull. It is possible to count strokes down the pool using this drill, as a measure of efficiency.

7. *Pull with a dolphin kick.* The emphasis of this drill is on arm pull, while using a dolphin kick to keep the hips up. The kick should be minimal to help develop the pull to its fullest.

8. *One-arm pull.* This drill is done to isolate the movement of each arm. The nonworking arm is extended out straight. The working arm does a perfect pull, concentrating on hand speed. This can be done with or without a kick. Be sure to work on both arms, as one will almost certainly be better at pulling than the other.

9. *Pop-up drill.* This drill exaggerates the acceleration of the hands across the body and the squeezing of the elbows under it. As the elbows squeeze, the body "pops up" as high and as playfully as possible out of the water. Repeat several times at the end of the pull, and try to get higher each time. Use with

a breaststroke kick. This motion lifts the shoulders out of the water in time for the force of the kick to be properly applied.

10. *Pull with a buoy*. Much breaststroke pulling should be done with a pulling buoy between the legs. Using a buoy increases resistance slightly, and allows you to concentrate on coordinating the efforts of both hands.

A quality start requires practice so that it is automatic by competition time.

2

Starts, Turns, and Finishes

Three important facets of competitive swimming that must be continually worked on are the start, turn, and finish of each racing stroke. Swimmers must ensure that their practice starts, turns, and finishes are performed in exactly the same manner that they will be during actual competition. Properly executing each of these movements requires attentiveness and concentration; if they are practiced properly, they will become more automatic during races. Your goal, then, when working on these three areas, is to practice them perfectly in order to make the action automatic. As with many skills, often you will have to make a conscious effort to perform starts, turns, and finishes properly, and you'll benefit if you develop a system of self-checks to nip any bad techniques in the bud.

In this chapter, we will take each stroke as a unit and describe the start, turn, and finish appropriate for each race. The techniques that will be described are those that are considered to be traditional. Each coach or experienced swimmer has personal variations that make the movement more efficient for him or her, and a number of teaching variations have evolved over the years. Presented here are those techniques widely considered to be excellent.

Each section is divided into a general description of the movement, a more detailed explanation with key words, and finally, tips to consider for greater efficiency.

THE FREESTYLE START

Over the past 20 years, the start in freestyle has evolved from a torpedo-like flat landing on the surface to a clean, "slick" entry through what swimmers term a "hole" in the water, thus greatly reducing the amount of resistance the body encounters on the entry and adding greater velocity and distance to the start. Almost all swimmers in individual events now use the "grab" starting position described below, and leap up and out at the starting signal. They then make the entry hands first, following in the same spot with the head, shoulders, chest, hips, and legs. After the entry, swimmers today adjust their body position quickly to the horizontal by using their hands as deflectors, then kick and time the first stroke to break the surface smoothly. Their goal at the start is to react quickly at the sound of the starting gun, enter the water smoothly, and gain maximum distance in a minimum period of time. Their velocity at entry is greater than at any other time during the race, and the best swimmers try to capitalize on this velocity.

Position

The proper starting position in the grab start is at the front of the block, with your toes curled over the lead edge of the block. Your body should be bent from the waist, so that your hands can grasp the lead edge of the block between your feet. Your feet should be a natural, comfortable distance apart, and your hips lined up so that each hip joint is directly above the corresponding ankle joint. Do not lean forward or backward. Your eyes should be looking slightly back between the legs; your knees and elbows should be slightly flexed.

The freestyle start: position on the block.
When assuming your position for the freestyle start, stand on the block with your toes curled over its front edge (A). In preparation for the start, grip the lead edge of the block between your feet (B).

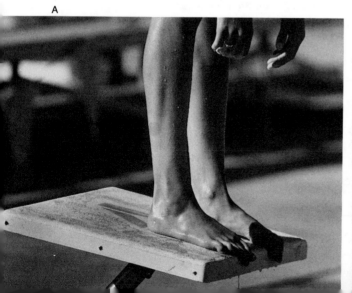

A

B

The Action

At the starting signal, you should perform a definite sequence of events for maximum efficiency:

1. *Your hands pull down* on the block, thereby starting your body toward the water.
2. *Your head snaps forward,* so that your eyes are looking down the course. This sets the course of your body out over the water.
3. *Your arms extend,* aim at the entry spot, and lock.
4. *Your legs spring,* providing maximum thrust to your body, which is now positioned to aim up and out over the water.
5. *Your head snaps down between your arms* and locks, and your upper arms touch the back of your head.
6. *You make your entry through one point (the entry spot) in the water.*
(SAFETY NOTE: It's possible to severely injure yourself if you attempt this dive in shallow water, or if you are not experienced at executing the dive, or if you are unfamiliar with the actual depth of the water. Before attempting this dive, you should practice under trained supervision, in deep water, until you can limit the maximum depth of your dive to less than 2 to 2½ feet if you are an adult and 2 feet if you are a child. Even then, you should not attempt the dive in less than 4 feet of water. Inexperienced swimmers can make dangerous mistakes here. If you are new to swimming, your learning effort should be carefully monitored, whether in deep or shallow water.)
7. *As your body enters the water, it is held in a streamlined position, and your hands adjust* to change the momentum from a diagonal direction to a strictly horizontal one. This has the effect of shooting the body forward in the water.
8. As your body shoots forward, you *time the beginning of your leg kick* to occur as the forward speed from your dive begins to dissipate.
9. After only a very short period of kick, the streamlined position is broken by the start of the *first arm pull.*
10. *Your first arm pull is timed so that the arm exits past the thigh cleanly through the surface of the water.*
11. You take your *first breath* somewhere *after two to four arm pulls,* depending upon your preference and the distance of the event.
12. You can consider your start *complete* when you have *established your arm stroke* and achieved a *high body position* in the water.

The Freestyle Start

A

When you hear the starting signal, pull down on the edge of the block and snap your head forward (A).

B

Now extend your arms forward as your legs spring. Your arms should aim at the entry point and lock (B, C).

E

F

Then your head snaps down between your arms and locks; your upper arms should touch the back of your head. Make your entry through one spot in the water (E, F).

C

D

Your legs should spring straight, providing maximum thrust to your body, which is aimed over the water (D).

**TIPS FOR THE
FREESTYLE START**

1. Train yourself to concentrate on the initial body movement, the *hands pulling down* on the block, rather than concerning yourself with when the starting signal will sound. You should *react* to the start signal, not be thinking about it. Concentrate on your hands.

2. Curl your hands around the front edge of the block with your thumbs forward, rather than with your thumbs in opposition to the fingers. That will enable you to react faster to the start signal.

3. The moment your legs enter the water, moving them in a single downward dolphin-like kick helps create additional forward speed on the dive.

4. Practicing a streamlined position as your body enters the water helps maximize the effect of the dive.

5. As your arms streamline, it's useful to place one hand on top of the other, with the bottom hand being that of the stronger arm, which will pull first. The top-hand thumb "locks" around the edge of the bottom hand to hold them together on entry.

6. On the dive itself, your legs should be kept firmly together and not allowed to "split" either vertically or horizontally on the entry. Your goal is maximum streamlining.

FREESTYLE TURNS

The turn in freestyle has undergone a number of variations over the years, and there are a great range of options currently in use. Let's look at two of the most popular ones.

In the first option, you approach the wall, and once you judge that your feet can reach it, you execute a front flip, going from a position on your front to a position on your back. You then use your feet to push off the wall in a streamlined position, with your arms extended overhead, and as you push off, you rotate onto one side, resume your kick, and stroke with your lower arm, which rotates the body back to the frontal swimming position as it breaks the water surface.

In the second option, which many people find simpler, you approach the wall as you did above, but instead of doing a straight front flip, you execute a shoulder roll, which, after throwing the feet to the wall for the push-off, puts the body immediately in the side position. In effect, this turn is a twist rather than a flip.

Either option is effective if executed properly, and by experimenting with each, you'll more than likely develop a preference for one over the other. Let's look at each in greater detail.

The Front-Flip Turn

You initiate the turn by leaving both hands at your hips following the last stroke with each hand. Turn your hands palm down, and assist the flip by pushing them toward the pool bottom as you drop your head to your chest and pike your hips upward, breaking the surface. Your hands remain in their extended position as your legs tuck tight to your body to aid in rapid rotation and then extend to the wall to plant and push off. Mechanically speaking, this leg extension is much like a forceful kick to the wall.

You are now on your back, and your arms are extended over your head. The back of your head should be tight against your biceps to allow for maximum streamlining. On the pushoff, the initial deceleration is the signal to begin a rapid kick and a quarter rotation to the side body position. Continue your kick, and as your speed slows down, time your first stroke to complete a smooth transition to the frontal position. Take your first stroke with your lower arm, and complete the rotation. The end of the stroke should smoothly exit the water. Then take anywhere from two to a dozen strokes before your first breath, depending on the length of the race and your personal preference.

There are two chief advantages to the flip turn:

1. It is a very powerful movement, with excellent speed potential.
2. It can get you deep in the water and out of the way of the turning waves of incoming swimmers and the wave off the wall.

Its chief disadvantage? It involves several movements—the flip, the kick, and two quarter rotations. These make it a somewhat energy-consuming turn.

The Front-Flip Turn

A

B

F

Start the flip turn by leaving your hands at your hips following the last stroke with each arm (A). Push your hands toward the pool bottom, palms down, and simultaneously tuck your head to your chest and pike your hips upward, breaking the surface with them (B). Tuck your legs tight to your body, which will cause you to rotate rapidly onto your back (C). Then extend your arms, find the wall with your feet, and push off (D). As you push off, you should rotate your body a quarter turn sideways and your hands should be in the streamlined position, one atop the other (E). After the push-off and the turn, take the first stroke with your lower arm, completing the rotation (F).

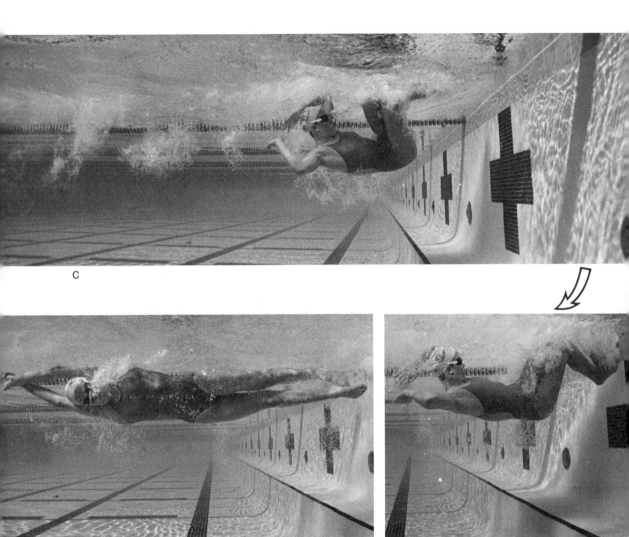

C

E

D

The Shoulder-Roll Turn

In this turn you approach the wall, and upon deciding when to initiate the turn, you leave your left arm back at the hip, with the palm facing the bottom of the pool. You are now positioned to begin a turn with your right shoulder. Tuck your chin close to your left armpit, and point your right shoulder toward the turning wall. As the right arm strokes, it finishes at the left hip, and as the legs tuck and extend to the wall, you slip the right hand under the left, which has assisted the turn by pressing down on the water. Your body should now be on its right side, and as your legs push off the wall, your kick and pull movements are the same as those for the flip turn. Placing the right hand under the left allows it to smoothly begin the first pull.

The advantages of the shoulder-roll turn?

1. *Simplicity.* Several complicated movements are eliminated, and it is easy to learn.
2. *Energy savings.* The energy you expend to execute the turn is substantially less than in the flip.

The chief disadvantage of the shoulder roll turn: It is not as easy to turn deeply with this movement. It is essentially a shallow turn, which means that you will find yourself in the midst of some surface water turbulence during short sprint races.

TIPS FOR FREESTYLE TURNS

Judging the wall's location and your approach speed is crucial, and can only be learned by trial and error. Gradually your perception of the nearness of the wall will improve and you'll make fewer mistakes.

Also, it's vital that you learn and practice extreme streamlining when leaving the wall. Most studies show that the ability to streamline accounts for up to 90 percent of the difference in the ability of various swimmers to turn rapidly. Your hands must be placed one on top of the other, with the upper thumb acting as a "lock" to hold them together. Your lower hand should always be the one to initiate the first pull after the turn. Your arms must be hyperextended and your head pressed tightly against the back of the arms and not between them, since that leads to a bulky and rather unstreamlined profile.

Two further tips: Your legs should "kick" at the wall, treating it as if it were a very hot surface that you want to get off of as quickly as possible. Never plant your feet for the pushoff; instead, extend them quickly and, in effect, "jump" off the wall.

Finally, establishing a breathing pattern and a high body position off the wall is an integral part of any turn. Restricting your initial breathing off the turn until you've achieved the desired high body position is good technique because it helps you establish the initial stroke rhythm, adds to speed off the wall, and keeps the body streamlined at a critical moment, further enhancing your speed.

THE FREESTYLE FINISH

Though relatively simple, the freestyle finish is a skill that should be repeatedly practiced at the end of each and every practice swim.

As you approach the wall, at some point you should decide to finish the race without taking any more breaths. At that point, your concentration should be directed totally onto the wall. Accelerate both your kick and your arm turnover, and drive to the wall, extending onto your side to elongate the body as much as possible. (Note: The human body is longer extended on its side than it is in a shoulders-square-to-the-wall position. Turn sideways and *extend*.) Make the touch itself with your fingertips, not with the palm of your hand, and keep your head in the water until the touch occurs, since lifting the head shortens the reach.

THE BACKSTROKE START

There used to be several versions of the backstroke start, based on differences in what the rules allowed. Short-course (USA) rules allowed the use of the stand-up start, with the toes over the edge of the gutter. This toe position was used in the more frequently seen in-water starts. International rules (FINA) preclude this starting position because the toes must be positioned below the surface of the water. In this section, we'll learn the international backstroke start, which is now used in US and NCAA competitions.

To position yourself for the start, assume a waiting stance with your body facing the starting wall, your toes below the surface of the water, and both hands grasping the bar on the starting block used for backstroke. On the command "Take your mark," pull yourself up into a crouched position, and at the crack of the starter's pistol, extend backward in a back jump. Your arms should reach for the water, and your body arch over it in a short back dive so that you enter in a streamlined position, hands first and hips up. By adjusting your hand pitch behind your head, you can manipulate the depth and distance of your dive just as you did for the freestyle start, and you can begin the kick and first pull at the desired time.

Starting Position for the Backstroke Start

Your feet can be placed in a variety of widths and depths, depending upon what's most comfortable for you. Place your hands on the starting bar (generally palms down), with your thumbs around the bar. Again, exact hand placement is a matter of personal comfort. Your body dimensions will dictate the

The backstroke start.
In accordance with long-course (international) rules, to position yourself for the backstroke start, enter the water, face the starting block, grasp the bar with both hands, and place your feet below water level against the wall at whatever width and depth feel

A

B

C

precise position you assume in relation to each different type of block you confront, and in general you must maintain a certain degree of mental flexibility to deal with what can be a wide variety of backstroke starting apparatus from one meet location to the next.

At the words "Take your mark," lift your body toward the block by pulling up, and move your head close to the block. Your body should be curled into the block as much as possible, ready to explode backward. You'll find that the angle of your body (back) to the starting wall cannot be too steep, or your feet will slip from the wall.

At the crack of the starter's gun, a precise series of events should take place:

1. Snap your head sharply backward.

2. Almost simultaneously, your hands push off the bar and swing out and around, with the palms turned up.

3. Now, lift your hips up and toward the starting bar, and begin to extend your legs.

comfortable to you (A). At the command "Take your mark," curl your body close to the wall (B). At the starting signal, snap your head backward (C) and push off the bar, swinging your hands out and around (D). Extend your arms and legs back in a straight line as you look for the entry hole (E). Streamline your body as it enters the water (F).

D

E

F

4. Keep extending your legs and dive backward over the surface of the water. The aim is to produce a single point of entry, through which your hands enter first, followed by your head, shoulders, torso, hips, and legs.

5. As you enter the water, the direction of your body will be determined by your hand position. You can attain greater depth by pitching the hands downward so that water pressure increases on the palms. You can make your dive more shallow by decreasing your hand pitch so that water flows on the backs of your hands. Head position also influences the depth of the start. The further back the head is tilted, the deeper the dive; the more the chin moves toward the chest, the shallower the dive.

6. As your body begins to slow down, start your kick and, finally, make your first arm pull to bring the body to the surface. Time this latter move so that the finish of the first pull results in a smooth exit from the water.

TIPS FOR THE BACKSTROKE START

1. Find the correct acute angle between the body and the wall for the best balance and pressure.

2. Your leg extension at the start should come late in the overall action

The underwater butterfly kick after the backstroke start.
Swimmers using the underwater butterfly kick as part of their backstroke start set a number of world records in 1988, but FINA (Fédération Internationale de Natation Amateur) has restricted the distance a backstroker may use the kick in international competitions to 10 meters. Currently no such restrictions exist for U.S. short-course or collegiate competitions, though it is likely that by 1991 all competitions here and abroad will adopt a 25-meter limit.

A

B
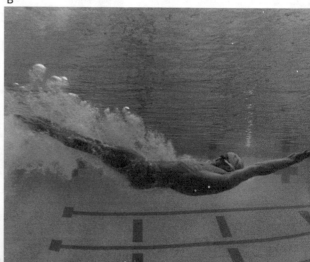

to ensure maximum backward pressure on the wall.

3. Streamlining is of utmost importance, as is the ability to judge when to begin your first stroke for a smooth transition. Streamline with your hands one on top of the other. In backstroke, however, remember that the hand that will pull first goes on the bottom.

4. Do not hang on the backstroke starting bar for long. This position will drain blood from your arms and fatigue them. Assume the position only when commanded, so that you maintain it for as short a time as possible. If there is a false start, drop into the water and relax your arms until the next start.

5. Lifting the hips toward the bar as much as you can on the start will always maximize your flight above the water and help ensure a smooth entry.

6. Some swimmers find they get greater speed and distance with a short series of double-leg butterfly kicks at the start instead of a series of backstroke flutter kicks. For good butterfly kickers, this is becoming an increasingly popular option.

With or without restrictions, the butterfly, or dolphin, kick can help you achieve some very fast times. To initiate this double-legged kick, perform a backstroke start, streamlining your body as you enter the water by overlapping your outstretched hands (A). Drop your hips (B) and then lift them quickly (C), working your legs from the thighs down like a giant fin (D). (See the butterfly stroke, page 52).

C

D

THE BACKSTROKE TURN

There are a number of ways to turn in the backstroke. Most methods are variations on the same general movement, with the variations inspired by differing anatomical considerations. Let's look at what might be called a "traditional" backstroke turn.

For this you approach the wall, locating it by counting your hand entries after your head passes under the backstroke flags. On the last stroke, you dive and reach for the wall. A combination of the hand pressure on the wall and the hand pressure in the water produces a spin action that reverses the direction of your head and upper body. Your legs then lift over the water surface to place themselves on the wall. You streamline, then push off the wall deep into the water, and extend your body, kick, and initiate the first stroke after the turn.

The Approach

You'll know the wall is near when your head goes under the backstroke flag. It is imperative that you learn exactly how many strokes it takes you to reach the wall from the flags. The safest way to count strokes is to count hand entries, each entry counting one stroke. For high-school-age swimmers, the usual count is three or four strokes. It is important that you accelerate your kick as you near the wall. That will keep your legs up in the water, and ready to lift and turn.

On the last stroke, dive backward toward the wall so that your lead hand contacts the wall 12 to 18 inches (or more) deep. Place your hand with your fingers toward the centerline of the body, in front of the head, and your thumb pointing up.

The Action

As your hand contacts the wall and "plants," your head follows in the direction of the turn. Your planting hand initiates the turn by pushing *toward the fingers.* At the same time, your free hand sweeps in a circle behind your head, completing the power for the turn. The palm of the free hand should keep pressure on the water throughout the action. Now lift your legs out of the water to place your feet on the wall, and direct your planting hand forward. Join your two hands behind your head and extend your body into a streamlined position. Once your body is streamlined, straighten your legs to push your feet off the wall, and adjust your body for depth in the same manner as you did on the start, using your hands as rudders. Begin your leg kick, either flutter or dolphin (butterfly), and finally, make your first arm pull with your stronger arm.

Hand Plant for the
Backstroke Turn

Your hand should touch the wall from behind
your head, with your arm fully extended (A).

A

At the moment of contact, your fingers should
point toward the center of the lane (B).

B

The Backstroke Turn

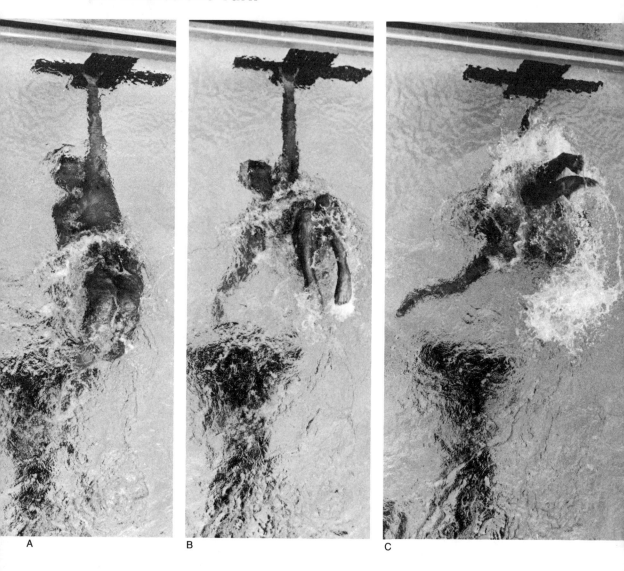

A   B   C

Once your extended hand has made contact with the wall, bend your knees to lift your legs from the water (A). The palm of your free hand should keep pressure on the water to assist the turn (B). Now lift your legs out of the water and place them on the wall, replacing your hand (C, D). Streamline your body by stretching your arms and overlapping your hands (E). Now push vigorously off the wall and prepare for your next stroke (F).

D   E   F

TIPS FOR THE BACKSTROKE TURN

1. Streamline before you push off the wall. If you streamline after the push, the power generated by your legs will already have been lost.

2. The deeper you plant your hand, the easier it will be for you to execute the turn.

3. Always push toward the *fingers* of the planted hand.

4. Always strive for long, deep turns to maximize speed off the wall and minimize body resistance.

5. Accelerating your kick into the wall will greatly enhance the speed of the overall turn and the ease with which your legs "come over" into the wall.

THE BACKSTROKE FINISH

Like the freestyle finish, the finish in the backstroke is a simple but vital action that needs daily practice. You will note that nowhere in the discussion of backstroke turning did I mention the idea of looking for the wall. The accomplished backstroke swimmer recognizes that there is nothing more destructive

The backstroke finish.
When performing a backstroke finish, your body should be rolled as far to one side as you can without your hips passing the invisible vertical line that defines the backstroke position. As in freestyle, you should "dive" for the wall and make the touch with the hand that's deepest in the water.

than head movement, both on the turn and on the finish. Whether turning or finishing, you *must* take your location clues from the backstroke flags.

In the backstroke finish, the approach is the same as in the turn; again, you count the hand entries after your head passes under the flags. As in freestyle, at some point you must make a commitment to stretch for the wall, and then dive and extend backward to touch the wall with your fingertips. Again, it is best to get as much on your side as the rules allow, without having your hips pass the vertical line that defines the backstroke position. You make the touch with the hand that is deepest in the water.

THE BUTTERFLY START

The butterfly start for both long- and short-course competitions is a fairly straightforward repetition of the freestyle start up until the point of entry. (In the start for the long-course competition, you begin back from the front of the block and step forward to the front edge at the command "Take your mark.")

The grab start position is the same as that for freestyle (see page 74). Upon entry into the water, it is normal to adjust the dive a bit deeper than in freestyle (assuming that water depth allows this to be done safely), and the legs execute a series of short, sharp kicks to bring the body to the surface.

After the entry, you then execute several short kicks to rise to the surface. Generally, younger swimmers take at least two complete kicks before their first arm stroke, and older swimmers take many more, depending upon individual preference. The key is to maintain excellent speed under the surface without jeopardizing oxygen requirements. The "breakout" stroke is extremely important; it must come smoothly through the surface. If you take this stroke too soon, it will result in the hands getting caught deep under the surface as the first stroke finishes. Timing this motion efficiently, therefore, requires practice. After you take the first stroke, keep your head down for at least one more stroke before taking a breath. Then take two full strokes before taking a breath on the third stroke. This breathing pattern is extremely important, because taking a breath right off the turn will result in your "standing up" into the first wave off the wall, and thus slowing down. Keeping your head down helps establish good body position for the rest of the length.

TIPS FOR THE BUTTERFLY START

1. The kick on the start should be short, sharp, and controlled.
2. Always maintain good streamlining during the underwater kicks.
3. Your head position helps determine when your body surfaces. Hold the back of your head parallel to the flat surface of the water until ready to come up, then smoothly lift it to push the face forward through the water. Be sure to lift *forward* as well as up. Think of pushing through the surface.

THE BUTTERFLY TURN

There is a rule difference in butterfly turns between short (25-yard) and long (50-meter) courses. In short-course butterfly competitions, you may lower one shoulder after completing the final arm pull. The wall touch does not have to be on the same horizontal plane, but it must be made with both arms simultaneously. (Theoretically, this makes it possible to do a flip-style butterfly turn, though to date, none has been seen consistently in competition.) In the more restrictive long-course rules, the turn must be done with the shoulders parallel to the water surface, though the hands may touch unevenly.

The Butterfly Turn: An Overview

The butterfly swimmer seeks to hit the turn with his arms comfortably extended at the end of a stroke cycle, to avoid either kicking to the wall or "jamming" the wall by approaching too close to it. This requires experienced judgment and considerable practice. As you touch the wall, make a 90-degree pivot to either side, and streamline your body as you leave the wall on your side. As you push off the wall, streamline and kick, then rotate another 90 degrees onto your chest, from where you resume the stroke. Most butterflyers take two strokes before the first breath after the turn in sprint events and one stroke in the 200 butterfly event—but individual variations are considerable.

The butterfly swimmer should try to "hit the turn" at full extension.

The Butterfly Turn:
Detailed Description

Stroke to the wall, keeping your kick going all the way to it. It is vital to keep kicking to maintain good body position. As your hands touch the wall, your head should reverse direction and look to the *side wall* of the pool. As it does so, the elbow of the first arm to come off the wall moves to the point of the hip, and the hand swings away from the wall, and deep, with the palm facing up, applying pressure to the water. (This helps bring the body down into the water.) Your feet plant on the wall as your other hand leaves it, and that hand travels behind your head to meet the first hand off the wall and overlap in a streamlined position. As your legs push off and your eyes are directed straight down, your body rotates 90 degrees, onto the chest. You then take two or three kicks to bring the body to the surface, and your first stroke breaks out smoothly through the surface. One more stroke and then you resume your breathing pattern for the next length.

The Butterfly Turn

A

Keep your kick working all the way to the wall.

F

Your body is streamlined and on its side as it pushes off the wall.

B

When your hands make contact with the wall, your head should be down.

C

As one hand pushes away from the wall, tuck your knees tight; this allows you to swing your feet toward the wall. The body becomes perpendicular to the wall.

E

Your other hand now enters the water just behind your head and streamlines to join your lower hand.

D

As your feet make contact with the wall, apply upward leverage with your free (lower) hand, helping your upper body rotate through the water.

TIPS FOR THE BUTTERFLY TURN

1. Counting strokes during the butterfly is critical in order to hit the wall properly, as well as to maintain stroke discipline. You'll find that your stroke count will change considerably when you shave your body for competitions, and you should note this count difference carefully.

2. Tucking your legs tightly into the turn will help your body rotate faster to the wall. Tucking one foot on top of the other will offer even more speed.

3. Keep your arms relatively extended from the wall during the turn. Bend your elbows enough to use your arms to push off, but not enough to push your face close to the wall. Remember: The body can't swim in any direction in the water until the head is out front.

4. Both hands and feet need to treat the wall like a hot plate and not linger. Get into and out of the turn FAST!

THE BUTTERFLY FINISH

The butterfly finish is simple. The only tricky part is judging the best touching method. The hands simply extend to the wall, and the head stays down, thereby affording the body the maximum amount of stretch. The hips and legs kick very hard to the finish, and the swimmer thinks of accelerating to the wall. This can be accomplished in several ways, the first of which is to take the last breath under the backstroke flags (or even farther out) and sprint to the wall (the desire for a breath will add a certain impetus to the finish). The second method is to change the stroke rhythm slightly by using the shoulder muscles to "pull" the arms forward in the recovery. (This can also be used as a stroke technique in sprint events, though only the very strong will use it successfully for long.) The touch itself is made with the head down, and the hands may be positioned at any of many different levels in both short and long course, though in the latter the shoulders must remain even.

THE BREASTSTROKE START

The starting technique for the breaststroke is similar to the other grab start techniques previously described. Where water depth is sufficient, there is some advantage in making the dive slightly deeper. When the dive velocity begins to decrease, you execute a "pullout," and this propels you a considerable distance down the length of the pool. The pullout consists of one kick and one pull; the following second kick must bring you to the surface. You may take a second pull before the head surfaces.

As you feel yourself begin to slow down, your extended arms should press out wide, then quickly in to the midline of the body, then snap through to the hips. Regarding timing, you should begin with the following sequence and then adapt for individual strengths and weaknesses: dive, entry, count (*one, two, three*) slowly. Then begin the outward press. After the hands snap to the hips, hold them right along the thighs, and count (*one, two*), and recover. The recovery should be with the hands very close to the body and the elbows tucked close to the side. Your head position is crucial: holding still, looking at the bottom of the pool throughout the pullout, until your hands pass your face on the recovery. At that point, your head should snap up as your hands begin the second stroke.

TIPS FOR THE BREASTSTROKE START

1. The OUT, IN, SNAP sequence should involve a steady hand acceleration throughout. The goal is to generate a sustained surge of power to propel the body rapidly through the water.
2. Streamlining the body is critical in all phases of the pullout.

THE BREASTSTROKE TURN

The breaststroke turn is similar to the butterfly turn. Here you must touch the wall with both hands on the turn, though they do not have to be at the same level. Your shoulders must be parallel to the surface of the water, and the turning mechanism itself is the same as described for the butterfly. When pushing off the wall, your body should be propelled either parallel to the water surface or very slightly down. At this point, you utilize the pullout mechanism just described. Count "one, two, three," from the time your feet leave the wall before initiating the pullout itself.

The Breaststroke Start

A

B

After you've performed a streamlined racing dive, begin the pullout for the breaststroke start by pressing outward with your hands.

After the press-out, your hands should accelerate through to the thighs, passing under the body.

The Breaststroke Turn

A

For the turn, concentrate on the wall and make the touch with both hands (A). One hand leaves the wall first, with that elbow passing the hip as your legs swing to the wall (B). Tuck your knees tight as your free arm swings outward (C). Just as in the butterfly turn, your body should be positioned on its side as it prepares to push off (D).

C

Your body should be perfectly streamlined in the water: hands at your sides, head down, legs straight, feet together.

Now start your recovery by drawing your hands in front of you in the streamlined fashion (one atop the other), keeping your elbows at your sides, and begin your next breaststroke, which should carry you to the surface.

B

D

THE BREASTSTROKE FINISH

Accelerate the stroke rate in the final meters and stretch on the finish, touching the finish pads with your fingertips. As on the turn, both hands must touch the wall simultaneously. Work on developing your timing so you always come to the wall (for both turn and finish) on the end of a *kick,* rather than on a pull, lest you must rush your hands back to the wall. Extend and touch.

THE INDIVIDUAL MEDLEY TURNS

The turns that make up the transition between the strokes play a vital part in the success of the individual medley (IM) swimmer. The additional turns that must be mastered are the butterfly-to-backstroke turn, the backstroke-to-breaststroke turn, and the breaststroke-to-freestyle turn. Once again, there are a number of different techniques that can be used, and those presented here are time-tested traditional turns. Personal experimentation may produce some modifications that will prove advantageous.

The Butterfly-to-Backstroke Turn

The end of the butterfly leg of the IM must follow the rules for butterfly, with your shoulders and hands parallel to the turning wall, as described earlier. As your two hands contact the wall, your lead hand should come off the wall first and drop underwater near the hip, then sweep out underwater with the palm up. Your head should continue to look at the turning wall as your body rotates back onto the lead-hand side. The body then sinks back down into the water, as the second hand leaves the wall with the palm of that hand facing the midline of the body. Your body should be on its side, with your head looking up to maintain the legal toward-the-back body position. The second hand joins the lead hand behind your head, with the hands aligned with the lead (or stronger) hand on the bottom so that it can pull first. Your legs then drive off the wall, and you streamline your body and kick your legs under the surface in a backstroke pushoff. The lower (strong) hand pulls first, which brings the lower side of the body to the surface, and the hand recovers smoothly into the first stroke.

The Backstroke-to-Breaststroke Turn

There are two equally respected standard procedures for this turn: the back-flip method and the open turn. Let's look at both.

The back-flip method. In this method you approach the wall, counting strokes as you do for a back turn or finish, and dive on the last stroke and make a deep hand placement on the wall. As your hand contacts the wall, flip your legs directly over your body, and assume a streamlined position as your feet replace the hand on the wall. Then push off into the breaststroke leg, executing the breaststroke pullout previously described, and begin the breaststroke swimming sequence.

The open-turn method. In this method you turn toward the wall on the last stroke, taking care not to roll the shoulder past the 90-degree vertical line, and roll your body onto its side as your hand touches the wall. Tuck your legs tight beneath your body and swing to the wall, as the "outside" hand (away from the wall) pushes up on the water to help reverse the body's direction. As your feet reach the wall, the hand on the wall goes behind your head and into a streamlined position behind your body as it streamlines and pushes off into the breaststroke pullout.

The Breaststroke-to-Freestyle Turn

This is a simple turn to execute. As you make the legal breaststroke touch at the wall, your lead arm reverses underwater, with the elbow at the point of the hip and the palm facing up toward the surface. Your head and body follow the lead arm into a position on the body's side. Your other hand goes behind the head and streamlines on top of the lead hand as described previously. Your legs then drive off the wall, kick, and you take the first freestyle stroke with your lower arm in order to maximize the stroke count taken with that arm and, not insignificantly, to bring your body up to the surface.

RELAY STARTS

Among the most exciting events in swimming are the various relay events. Each is truly a team effort, and many great moments in the history of swimming occurred during memorable relays when an underdog team came up with a totally unexpected victory. Throughout most of swimming history, the point scores for relays have been double that of individual events, which accurately describes the relays' historical importance.

The Backstroke-to-Breaststroke Turn

A

B

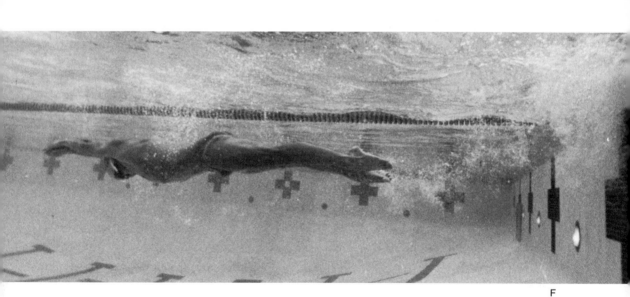

F

To perform this turn during the individual medley, you should know the number of strokes it takes you to reach the wall after you pass the overhead signal flags. Start counting when you pass the flags (A). On your last stroke to the wall, drop your arm deep and dive (B). As your palm touches the wall, flip your legs directly over your body (C), and tuck to complete the flip (D). Streamline your hands as your feet touch the wall (E). Push off in this streamlined position, ready to take your first breaststroke (F).

C

E

D

The Breaststroke-to-Freestyle Turn

A

F

E

This turn starts with a (legal) two-handed wall touch (A). Pivoting on your left hand, bring your legs up in a tuck (B, C) so that you are in a position to touch the wall with your feet (D). Note how the lead (lower) hand is facing upward, toward the water surface, and the upper hand is starting to come over the head to streamline with the lower one. Your body should be on its side as the hands streamline and the legs drive off the wall (E). With a kick (F), you are ready to take your first freestyle stroke.

B

D

C

The relay start technique is radically different from the grab start used today (and described earlier), and the overall timing of the transition between incoming and outgoing swimmer is vital in relay success. Winning teams spend hours perfecting their timing in the relay exchange. The rules require that the incoming swimmer legally touch the wall while the outgoing swimmer still has contact with the starting platform. This means that even only the outgoing swimmer's toe can be in contact with the block, while the rest of his body can already be out over the water. It should be clear, then, that the team with the best timing will gain a substantial advantage in the course of a relay race.

There are specific techniques that should be followed by the incoming and outgoing swimmer. If these are adhered to, the exchanges should be consistently fast and disqualifications relatively few. Let's look at these techniques from the point of view of each of the swimmers.

Start Procedure for the Outgoing Swimmer

The outgoing swimmer uses a windup start, which is a totally different technique from the grab start. The grab start is designed to get the athlete moving instantaneously, and into the water quickly. The windup start is designed to allow the swimmer to utilize the rules to get as long a dive as possible, with the greatest possible momentum, to thus accelerate his entry speed and force. The grab start serves no useful purpose in a relay event.

To execute a windup start, first sight down your arms to the shoulders of the incoming swimmer. You do this by imagining a line extending from your eyes to your fingertips to the other swimmer's shoulders. As the incoming swimmer approaches, keep visual contact with your fingertips and the swimmer's shoulders, and in effect "follow the swimmer into the wall." This step is vitally important since it helps you concentrate on the speed of the approaching swimmer and also helps you pick up the rhythm of her stroke. This is especially critical in the butterfly and breaststroke. By following the swimmer in this manner, your hands gradually lower as she approaches the block. As your hands lower, flex your knees and begin to bend your body at the waist until your upper body comes roughly parallel to the water. As the incoming swimmer's shoulders cross the "T" marked on the bottom of the pool, swing your arms back, then forward, straight out and full past the head and "underneath" the shoulders, the force of the swing aiming you down the pool. As the arms make that initial backswing, your body begins to fall toward the water, and your body weight shifts far forward. Timing this movement well results in a tremendous force of momentum off the block. Try to time your jump to capitalize on this momentum. If you follow this sequence properly and time it right, the incoming swimmer will have taken her final stroke and gotten her hand to the wall. (The incoming swimmer must follow her own set of instructions for this to work properly!) When swinging your arms forward, you must remember to forcibly stop them when your hands are pointing at the desired point of entry into the water. If the arms swing out unchecked, your momentum will be directed upward and the advantage of the windup start is lost.

The procedures for the outgoing swimmer can be summarized as follows:

1. Follow the swimmer to the wall using the extended-fingertip method.
2. When the incoming swimmer's shoulders cross the "T," wind up and go.
3. Don't look back! (No hesitation.)

Start Procedures for the Incoming Swimmer

Despite what it sometimes looks like to spectators, almost all disqualifications on relay starts are caused by some inconsistency in the finish of the incoming swimmer. Strict discipline must be observed by both incoming and outgoing swimmers if the start is to be optimal.

The incoming swimmer must:

1. Accelerate to the finish wall. No slowing down at the finish!
2. Take no more breaths after the backstroke flag (last 5 meters). Inhaling changes the rhythm of the stroke. By not inhaling, the incoming swimmer will accelerate and her final strokes will be uniformly strong.
3. Stretch that last stroke to the wall. No short strokes! At the point where the incoming swimmer must choose whether to stroke or stretch, she must always choose to stretch. More false starts are caused by swimmers who decide to take "just one more stroke" than by all other factors combined.
4. Kick very fast to the wall. Leg acceleration greatly aids the stretch-to-the-wall process.
5. Touch underwater. Underwater is the shortest, simplest way to the wall.

If both incoming and outgoing swimmers follow these simple guidelines, the quality of the team's relay starts will be both excellent and consistent. As the swimmers practice relay exchanges together, they will become accustomed to each other's personal moves and abilities, and their starts will begin to assume championship caliber!

Start Procedure for the Outgoing Swimmer

If you are an outgoing swimmer in a relay, prepare for your windup start by sighting down your arms past your fingertips to the shoulders of the incoming swimmer (A).

As the incoming swimmer's shoulders pass the "T" on the bottom of the pool, start your windup, swinging your arms back, then forward, straight out past the head and below the shoulders (B).

The arm swing under the shoulders adds momentum to help carry you farther in your start (C).

If your timing has been correct, the incoming swimmer's fingers will touch the wall as your toes leave the starting block (D).

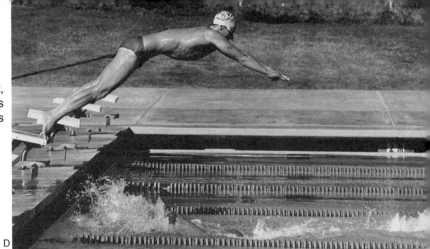

D

You then complete your dive using the proper entry technique (E, F, G).

E

F

G

3

Training

The basics of training the body for competitive swimming are very simple: Condition the muscles, cardiovascular system, and nervous system to perform at the levels desired to produce a certain speed. If you increase the capability of any one system, the potential is there for the improvement of the whole.

The key word here is "potential." Though increasing the capacity and capability of any one system will *allow* for improvement, the actual improvement results only from a delicate balancing of the different systems. Training, in a word, is *complex.* It is not our intent in this chapter to detail the scientific basis for all types of training. Rather, we will describe the key areas and functions of training, and discuss how they relate to the total training of the individual.

As we begin, we should note several considerations:

First, we must ask ourselves the question, "Training for what?" All of the effects of physical training are specific, and the concept of *specificity of training* is one of the first ideas we will tackle. One does not simply "train," one trains with a particular end in mind. That may be general conditioning, or it may be to swim a 100-yard freestyle in 41 seconds. But there must be an object, goal, or purpose to any training. Whatever form of training we utilize, it will very specifically prepare us for something. We must understand the concept of specificity if we are to train effectively.

Second, we must realize that training is *developmental.* By that we mean that appropriate training at age 10 with no background is inappropriate training at age 18 with 8 years of background. As we grow older and more experienced in swimming, we must modify what we do if we are to continue to progress. This is only logical, given that we change and mature as people. At the other

113

The specificity rule says that to prepare properly for your event, you must spend a significant amount of time preparing to swim at the speed required by the event.

end of the spectrum, we must recognize that, as we become masters athletes, the body changes once again and has different needs.

Third, training is based on the principle of *adaptation.* We systematically apply limited and planned stress to the body, and it builds and strengthens its capacity to respond to the stress. It's worth remembering that rest plays as vital a part in training as does stress, because the growth and strengthening of the systems occur during rest, not during stress. Rest is a basic ingredient in training.

Fourth, effective training is based on consistency of effort. It is without value to train intensely and vigorously for short periods of time and then detrain for a period of time and then reinvest in training. While rest is vital during training, long-term development is contingent on limited "break" or rest periods surrounded by long periods of consistent training and adaptive rest. Consistency counts! The champion is the athlete who can put in effective training over the longest period of time. Development of physical systems is progressive. Therefore, consistent application of stress and rest is the key to training.

With these general principles in mind, let's move on to a closer examination of the idea of *specificity of training.*

SPECIFICITY OF TRAINING

Specificity of training says that a person must train for the specific criteria that will be seen in the desired competition.

No ice skater would prepare for ice skating by pole vaulting. No NFL running back would prepare for the upcoming season by water skiing. Similarly, no sprint swimmer should prepare for a 41-second, 100 freestyle by swimming exclusively long, slow distance swims.

As we will discuss later, all forms of swim training are needed to some degree by all types of swimmers. The degree is determined by the nature of the events. We generally categorize swimming events by time designations:

• Sprint events are those events taking roughly a minute or less. These include the 50s and 100s.

• Middle-distance events are those that require roughly 1 to 3 minutes. These are the 200-yard events. In recent years, the 400-yard or -meter events have been considered more middle than long distance.

• Long-distance events are those requiring more than 4 minutes, which would be the 800-meter, 1000-yard, 1500-meter, and 1650-yard freestyle events,

plus those specific long-distance events held in open water competitions. In the
modern swimming era, 400-yard or -meter events lie in between the middle- and long-distance events.

The concept of specificity says that to prepare properly for each of the above events, you must spend a significant amount of training time preparing to swim at the speed required by the event. One of the great questions in modern training is "How much specific speed is enough?" We know that overdoing the specific training can lead to overtraining, staleness, and declining performances. Workouts that are not specific enough in speed will not achieve optimum training effect for competition.

Specific to what? Specific to speed of motion. To swim a 100-yard freestyle in 40 seconds, you must average 10 seconds per lap for the four-lap race. Given 1 second "credit" on the first lap for the dive, you must effectively swim the remaining three laps in an average of 10 seconds. When doing specific race training, if you are training at slower than 10.33 seconds, you are specifically training to swim a 100 at slower than 40.2 seconds. It may not be that precise a measurement, but it's pretty close.

The key item in training specifically is providing energy to the muscles. This chemical energy is delivered by a variety of systems set up within our bodies. The systems overlap, and one system does not totally shut down the instant the other starts. It's more like a gradual shift from one to the other, as the demands of the body's performance increase. Without creating a small chemistry text here, it's important for us to have some understanding of these systems to grasp the concept of specificity.

ENERGY SYSTEMS

All muscular action (which propels the swimmer) is developed at the level of the individual muscle cell. The chemistry that takes place within the cells provides the energy to contract the individual cells, and the swimmer "recruits" these cells to create increasingly powerful muscular action as greater speed is required (this "recruitment," of course, is an automatic act).

There are two major chemical systems within which energy is produced. These are the *aerobic* and *anaerobic* systems. Aerobic means, simply, "with oxygen," and anaerobic, "without oxygen." The anaerobic system actually has three different subsystems to produce energy under differing time and "pressure" situations, and we will discuss these further. All of these systems wind up producing an energy unit known as ATP, which is then used by the individual cells as fuel.

The Aerobic System

When the energy demand of the body in either training or competition is low enough, there is sufficient oxygen entering the system through the lungs to allow aerobic production of ATP. This allows the body to continue in a chemically balanced state, and to continue the level of activity for a lengthy period of time. All long-distance events are swum predominantly in the aerobic state, using aerobically produced energy for the muscles. However, as any long-distance swimmer knows, there comes a time when the body begins to "burn" and the muscles begin to experience discomfort. Why? At a certain rate of activity, not enough oxygen can be supplied to produce the required energy, and there is a gradual shift to the anaerobic source of energy supply.

The development of the aerobic system is of vital importance in training. One of the key limiting factors in performance is how fast a swimmer can swim while still using the aerobic system. Once the swimmer moves substantially into the anaerobic system, it is a matter of time before the chemical level of the muscles becomes so acidic that further contraction is impaired, and a slowdown occurs (the anaerobic system creates lactic acid in the muscles, producing a characteristic "burning" sensation).

Development of the aerobic system is similar to the development of many other systems within the body. It's necessary to stress the aerobic system by swimming as much distance as possible at a speed that is borderline between aerobic and anaerobic. This is called *threshold training.* If a swimmer trains a bit too fast, he trains the anaerobic system. If he trains too slowly, he gains only a very limited aerobic benefit. Lactate testing (so called for the analysis of lactic acid, the substance produced as the by-product of the anaerobic system) is the current scientific method for determining the precise range of speed at which an individual needs to swim to achieve threshold training. In short, the development of the aerobic system is accomplished by subjecting the system to a slight overload and then allowing it to rest. The body will make minute chemical adjustments to adapt to the stress, and will shift the "threshold point" to a slightly higher speed.

One of the key points to recognize in long-term development of the athlete is that the young athlete, aged 11 to 15, is best able to significantly improve the production of the aerobic system. In older athletes major shifts

Compared to swimmers in older age groups, young swimmers are best able to improve their aerobic systems for swimming—or for any other sport.

will occur, but not as easily nor as permanently as in the younger athlete. Ideally, then, the young swimmer should acquire a superb aerobic base during the years 11 to 15.

This point is reinforced by the observation of the history of distance swimming. While there has been stagnation in the recent decade, the decade prior was filled with a seemingly endless stream of young teenage wonders demolishing the world records in the distance events at a fantastic rate. During the past 10 years, we have been preoccupied with the idea that swimmers must "mature" later in the sport, and we have transmitted that idea into lower-yardage-and-intensity programs for younger swimmers. We have concurrently seen a national decline in distance swimming, while other nations have continued to experience some success with young distance athletes. Should we perhaps conclude that utilizing the potential for tremendous aerobic gains at an early age may be the key to improved distance swimming performance?

Maybe, but culturally this creates a problem. Traditionally, one of the major methods of conditioning swimmers aerobically has centered around increasing their training mileage. This *may* be undesirable from the point of view of retaining athletes in the sport (see the discussion under *Competition and Beyond*, page 213). It's possible that with our new scientific analysis of threshold training by means of the lactate analyzer, we may be able to refine and pinpoint training to a point where massive mileage will not be the only successful way to develop aerobic capacity.

The Anaerobic System

The anaerobic system produces ATP units without utilizing oxygen. Obviously the swimmer does not stop breathing when this system becomes predominant during a race! The oxygen consumed is simply not sufficient to fuel all the muscle fibers that are necessary to contract at high speed. The anaerobic system is divided into two subsystems that operate at different "demand levels" of the muscle cell. Each has its "assigned speed range" and a limited duration within which it can operate.

It may be helpful to think of these two systems as first and second gears in an automobile. First gear is necessary up to a certain speed. In swimming, this is between 0 and 30 seconds of speed (sprint) activity. It's important to note that swimming has almost no events that are completed within this time limit (the exception is the 50 freestyle). Some training of this system is necessary for sprint swimmers, however, as it will produce ATP for that limited period of time.

"Second gear" operates from 30 seconds to approximately 2½ minutes, and most swimming events are contested within this period. The longer events are predominantly aerobic, except for the finishing acceleration, as previously discussed.

Attaining specific speeds through training, and accumulating the appropriate amount of rest between training swims, are keys to the development of the anaerobic system. Both factors are essential in training the correct energy system. If too slow a speed is maintained in training, the appropriate "gear" is not stressed, and that energy system fails to develop. If too little rest is taken between efforts, again, the wrong system will do the training. As a generalized training guideline, first-gear training requires a 3:1 or 4:1 ratio of rest to work. For example, a succession of 50-yard freestyle swims (which swimmers call "repeat-50s") swum at, say, 30 seconds each, require 1½ to 2 minutes of rest between swims. One simple way to train first gear, particularly if one is training with a team, is to swim 50s in groups of heats. If each heat takes close to 30 seconds to swim, four heats will be concluded every 2 minutes and require 6 to 8 minutes of rest before the next four heats.

Training the second gear requires a rest-to-work ratio of 2:1. In this formula, swimming distances in groups of three (three heats) will do the job. Note that swimming 50s on a 2:1 rest-to-work ratio or less will simply result in slower practice times and, again, will train the second gear.

In short, the *intensity* of the effort coupled with the amount of *recovery time* determines which gear is being trained. And remember, all of this "training" consists, in reality, of minute changes in chemical composition and energy-source generation within each muscle cell. These chemical changes are based specifically on the systems we change, all of which relates back to our principle of *specificity* of training.

Next we will discuss the principle of developmental training, and explore what is necessary at each age and stage of athletic development in order for any swimmer to make reasonable and satisfying progress.

DEVELOPMENTAL TRAINING

One of the key principles in training is that it should be developmental in nature. This means that to train the swimmer optimally, at each stage of a swimmer's development different things should be emphasized. The training that is proper and appropriate for the college-age swimmer is not appropriate for the 10-year-old, even in scaled-down form. The young swimmer is not a miniature of the adult swimmer. Respecting this idea, all training must be geared to develop the swimmer appropriately.

Another important concept to remember is that all athletes develop individually. What one person can learn at age 7 another might not be ready to learn until 10. What one 14-year-old may be ready to do in training, another may not be ready to do until several years later. People develop in all things at different rates. This is true in swimming as surely as in school, music lessons, or any other learning situation. In short, we must come to expect in ourselves and others differing rates of development.

Developmental training for swimming should emphasize several areas. The first is aerobic training: training within the oxygen system. The second is anaerobic training and the first-gear, second-gear variations of sprint training previously discussed. A third is the biomechanics of strokes, starts, and turns. Other areas of emphasis include developing appropriate attitudes and specific knowledge. Though not strictly "training," they are, as we'll see, necessary to a complete and satisfying swimming experience.

The process of development is complex and individual, but there are certain guidelines to follow for a progression of successful training. These generalized guidelines are presented below. Keep in mind that these are *general* and that specific swimmers may be ready to progress more or less quickly depending on their individual rates of physical maturity and emotional and intellectual devlopment.

Training for Young Swimmers (Ages 6 to 10)

As a general guideline, the idea at this age is to go as fast as possible, for as long as possible, on as little work as possible. The key is to allow the youngster to learn to enjoy the sport while experiencing some success at improving times for events and improving technique. The most significant part of the training program should be learning stroke mechanics. Every yard swum correctly establishes good habits and correct neuromuscular patterns. Every lap swum incorrectly establishes bad habits that are difficult to unlearn and may quickly become lifelong disadvantages.

The next most significant part of the program for young swimmers is to begin to establish positive attitudes toward health, exercise, swimming, and "challenge" that will mold him or her as a competitive swimmer in the years to come. The chapter on swimming philosophy (Chapter 8) expands on this thought.

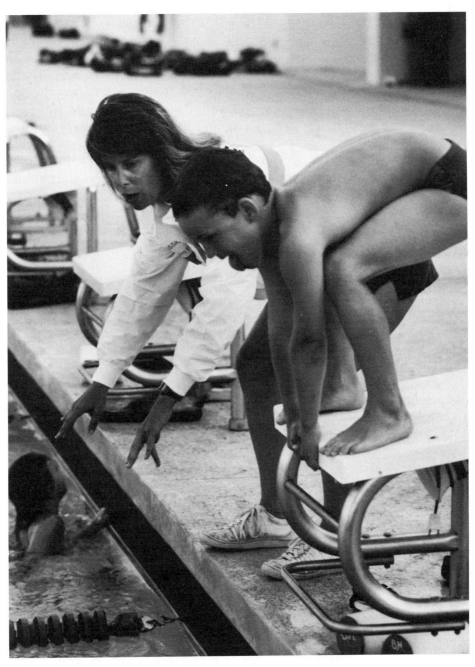

Young swimmers' workouts should be a blend of work and play.

The third significant facet of training at the younger ages is the actual swimming training itself. This should be primarily aerobic in nature: that is, the young swimmer's goal should be to learn to swim increasing distances with excellent stroke mechanics. Young swimmers do enjoy swimming fast, and short sprints in moderation can also be a fun and exciting part of the program. An often-neglected part of early swim training is opportunities for free play. The motion of sculling, for example, is vital to good stroke mechanics and skilled swimming, and it can best be developed at an early age through frequent opportunities for supervised and unsupervised water play. Games with balls or toys require quick bursts of speed, acceleration, and sudden starts and changes in direction. Such games are excellent at teaching youngsters the "feel for the water" that coaches discuss so much. So play time mixed with structured learning experiences provides the ideal mix for young swimmers.

Training in the Middle Years (Ages 11 to 14)

These are transition years. Each swimmer will, at some time during these years, undergo considerable physical changes associated with puberty, and the range of physical development will be a full and diverse one. Physiologists will insist that these are the key years to improve the condition of the aerobic energy system. The trick is to improve cardiovascular condition without falling into what swimmers call the "mileage trap." Through scientific training programs it's possible to elevate the function of the aerobic system to the necessary degree without exorbitant mileage in the pool. A special note is in order here. It's possible to produce fast times in young swimmers by increasing their mileage to an accelerated degree. It's been done in the past, and any coach can try to succeed at it, but there are serious long-term dangers in this approach. Early high-yardage programs can produce shoulder imbalance and shoulder soreness in the young swimmer that will hinder him throughout his career. It can also produce boredom with training—training burnout—that can lead to an early departure from the sport. In American society, it's difficult for any athlete to train much beyond 5 hours a day. If high-mileage, long-hour programs are begun too soon, maintaining the kind of improvement that produces motivation over a long swimming career will be nearly impossible. The aim, then, is to make efficient use of aerobic training through application of a scientific balance of intensity and duration of swimming and rest. A second aim is to improve the swimmer's biomechanics by improving his strokes, starts and turns. Third, attitudinal and intellectual concerns increase the more the swimmer becomes involved in the sport. Finally, a certain amount of work will be both physically and psychologically beneficial.

The priorities, then, are:

1. aerobic development,
2. stroke development,
3. attitudinal development,
4. sprint training.

Training in the High School Years (Ages 14 to 18)

Training during high school years takes a distinct shift. As the physical body matures, there is real opportunity to develop increasing strength, which results in more power and greater speed. Dry-land and pool strength training introduced in these years can play an important developmental role. Too, as the swimmer grows older and more mature, he can spend more time each season on anaerobic training and sprint swimming. The anaerobic system must have certain levels of enzymes and hormonal activity to develop significantly, and the high school years are when it can first make substantial improvements. Each season must also devote a portion of time to continued improvement and maintenance of the swimmer's aerobic system. As the aerobic system is brought into peak form early in the season, then improvement can come from development of the swimmer's anaerobic system.

Biomechanics (stroke mechanics) are still important in the high school years, but if they have been properly learned early in the swimmer's career, by the time he reaches high school, they need only to be polished and "reminded" for high performance levels. Of course, if the strokes do need adjustment, they should be attended to immediately.

Another cautionary word here about biomechanics: Just as physical development evolves over time, so will the stroke mechanics of the individual. The kid swimming butterfly at age 10 is small and lightweight, with one set of limb ratios, while the same kid at age 16 will be bigger, stronger, heavier, with different limb ratios and physical capabilities. His stroke, like that of any swimmer, will change somewhat over time. Maintaining good biomechanics is important, but trying to maintain the *same* biomechanics is nearly impossible and probably even detrimental to development.

Dry-land training for the high school–age swimmer and older is covered in Chapter 5. It's important to note, however, that roughly the same principles of development that are true in the water are true on land. Early strength training should emphasize high repetitions with low weights. Later, more resistance with fewer reps can be effective, but the idea generally in dry-land training for the high school–age swimmer is to do as little as possible for as long as possible, so long as she makes adequate progress. And remember, nothing destroys motivation more than lack of progress!

College-Age Training

College and post-college swimming are tremendously exciting for a swimmer, real rewards at the end of the swimming career. At the college level, development is coming to a peak, and all the years of preparation are paying off in the best performances the swimmer has ever had.

College swimmers have many good things going for them. Training, occurring as it usually does in late afternoon, is convenient and the pool on campus is usually easy to get to. The college swimmer is training with his peers, who in most cases are relatively close to his own abilities and interest level, and he is physically capable of tremendous performances. He is usually provided with excellent coaching, along with all the support facilities to make for the best athletic experience. True, the college swimmer faces the pressure of academic stress and a social environment that is not always conducive to dedicated training, but on balance the dedicated college swimmer is in a wonderful situation for personal development.

The actual training of college swimmers is not significantly different from that of high school swimmers, except that in most cases the work done is more a process of refining rather than learning, with an emphasis on training consistency. The swimmer has the physical tools at this level. His challenge is to apply himself consistently so that he might excel.

The principle of developmental training is quite simple: There is a time for each type of training that is optimal. The athlete will best benefit by applying the particular type of training at the proper time. It is possible to make artificial gains by misapplication of the principles during brief periods in one's career, but this will likely result in highly unsatisfactory long-term consequences.

The career of an athlete in all respects—and especially his or her developmental training—is best guided by a professional swimming coach. The long-term bond between a professional coach and a dedicated and determined athlete is the only "magic formula" in developmental swim training. Nowhere is this formula more important than in the principle of adaptation, the art of mixing stress and rest.

College swimmers seek to refine their technique and develop a high level of consistency.

ADAPTATION

All physical training is based on the simple idea of adaptation—the ability of the body to meet the challenges that are put to it. Each individual muscle, indeed each individual cell, makes chemical, and in the case of the muscle, structural changes to accommodate the needs of the athlete. The body literally changes itself to become as productive as the demands placed upon it.

This process of adaptation, then, is based on two simple variables: the first is *stress*, the second is *rest*. The entire process of training is dependent on developing the proper mix of these two properties. If you place too much stress on the body's systems, they will become chronically fatigued—"stale" or "over-trained"—and they will perform poorly and recover very slowly between efforts. If you rest too much throughout your program, your development will be slow, and your progress toward a highly trained state sporadic. If you rest too much after being in a highly trained state, you will rapidly lose some training benefits you have gained.

Stress

Stress is produced in two ways. The first is voluntary, during what we call the training process. The second is involuntary, and is caused by a number of factors which we will explore. Voluntary stress occurs when we get in the pool and swim. As we have already discussed, the various sets, interval training, and varieties of aerobic and anaerobic training that we utilize in our swimming program are designed to "push" the chemistry of energy production to its limits. This excess of demand over performance produces the stress necessary for improvement. Involuntary stress is less desirable, but it's a critical factor that you must consider in your training process. Environmental types of involuntary stress include:

Weather: In some parts of the world, winter cold is a definite stressor on the body's systems. If you live in such a climate, you must consider cold weather when you train, and even more important, you must educate yourself to recognize and cope with weather stressors. Clearly, the stifling heat of midsummer is equally stressing, and you should take adequate steps to protect yourself from dehydration when both training and competing. In short, any extreme weather condition is a challenge for the body and must be compensated for in the training equation.

Illness: Any form of illness is a system stressor. It is simply not possible to recover overnight from an illness, and the stress of even a simple cold will affect your performance in both training and competition.

School: If you're a college-age swimmer or younger, the energy that you expend in school-related activities is considerable. Worry over exams, school performance, and maintaining adequate homework time is a real stressor. Later we'll examine how to reduce these stressors, particularly when preparing for competitions.

Emotional stress: One of the most debilitating forms of stress is caused by emotions of any sort, either positive or negative. Extreme happiness is just as stressful as sadness. In young athletes, this problem can take innumerable forms and can be a major factor in performance. One of the keys to enhancing your swim performances is to learn to control and direct these emotions.

Stress, then, is necessary for training adaptation to occur, and can be both positive and negative. In order to train effectively, you must try to maximize the stress that comes from swim training and minimize unnecessary stress that arises from factors outside of training.

Rest

Rest is a period of consolidation and repair for the body. The body repairs itself in a way that makes the stressed system "more worthy" for future challenges. It compensates for the stress, making a repair that is *stronger* than the original, and thus the body is prepared to withstand even greater stress the next time.

This overcompensated (or super-compensated) repair takes place *only when a sufficient period of nonstressful time is allowed before the next stress.* This is an important fact to grasp, because if not enough rest is allowed, the body can only compensate itself incompletely, and the next applied stress will deepen the stress effect. Performance will steadily decline because the body is being constantly torn down with insufficient recovery. Adequate rest must be provided for the adaptation principle to take effect.

What is rest?

The most substantial way that the human body rests is in sleep. Nobody truly understands all the facets of the sleep mechanism, but all researchers agree that the quiet state of sleep is the key component to stress reduction and adequate rest. This has very important training implications. If the normal adolescent requires 7 to 8 hours of sleep a night, then the adolescent swimmer would be wise to balance his training stress by sleeping 8 to 10 hours per night. Unfortunately, modern American society rarely allows this luxury.

The average adolescent is in school from 7 to 8 hours per day. If she trains for 2 to 3 hours more, eats for a total of an hour, has miscellaneous transportation requiring another hour, and studies for another hour or two, she's left with a maximum of 9 hours to sleep, socialize, and otherwise enjoy life. As you can see, if you're an adolescent swimmer, you must develop time management skills if you are to get adequate rest.

At the very least, rest needs to be a period when your body has a break from physical activity and your muscle cells have a chance to work their magical chemical rejuvenation. As we shall discuss next, the concept of rest can be both absolute and, in the case of training itself, relative.

As we have seen, stress alternates with rest to produce adaptation. This process is the very essence of training. Swimmers and coaches working at the elite level spend a considerable amount of time planning their training program to reflect the perfect mix of stress and rest. Athletes and coaches at any level can follow these same steps, given the commitment to follow a prearranged training plan.

At the most elite echelons, Olympic athletes and those dedicated to high levels of performance will work from a 4-year (quadrennial) plan that structures the individual years in terms of high and low stress. The year following the Olympic games is typically a low-stress, high-rest year. In many cases, the next year will include an increase in stress and possibly a major international competition, such as the World Championships, which provides a meaningful way to evaluate the swimmer's training. The third year of the quadrennial is usually less stressful than the second year, but the baseline of training is still considerably higher than the first year of the plan. The fourth year is an all-out effort to attain the highest goals that the athlete can aspire to. This is simply an enlarged rest, work, rest-to-a-lesser-degree, work-very-diligently plan for training.

Below the elite levels, coaches and swimmers typically devise a plan that allows major rest after major conditioning, followed by alternating periods of relative work and relative rest during the course of the season and ending with a very substantial rest period prior to the major competition. Following each cycle of rest, the work level is raised above the previous work cycle (the work intensity increases), and generally the next rest cycle is less pronounced.

Every coach has his or her own preferred formula for the appropriate work/rest ratios, and most coaches recognize that no one answer is appropriate for all their swimmers. The very best coaches provide a cycle that accounts for individual differences of adaptation.

This cycle of work and rest carries right down to the weekly training plan, where coaches alternate work and rest and may even cycle the different types of work stress that they impose on the swimmer's body. In modern swimming,

Stress followed by rest produces adaptation.

perhaps the most crucial bit of the equation is not how much or what kind of stress to apply, but how much and what kind of rest to provide. There is considerable evidence that the socialist or Eastern Bloc countries that have made such substantial swimming progress in the past decade have concentrated hard on providing enhanced rest and recovery for their athletes, to allow them to spend increasing amounts of time in stressful training. If this is true, the key to future great swimming may reside in finding the keys to accelerated training recovery.

TRAINING CONSISTENCY

A review of the results of age-group swimming over a 35-year period shows that consistency is the one nonvariable in the careers of the great swimmers.

Recently sports science has validated this point. Studies have shown that in the development of athletes, long breaks from training are detrimental to high-level performance. The long-term goal, as suggested under the section on adaptation, is the continuous rise in the base level of physical conditioning. Successive seasons of increasing stress, followed by short breaks, result in this rise of base level. Indeed, most studies show that on a weekly basis, the best physical improvement results from frequent, relatively short training sessions, rather than a few very long sessions. The body responds better to frequent stimulating stress and complementary rest than it does to a few overwhelming sessions. Once the body is in a state of considerable fatigue, going deeper into fatigue is of no benefit whatever.

If you wish to achieve your personal best, you must understand that no one workout, week, month, or even year will make or break application of the other principles of training over a long period of time. You must have a training plan that takes into account the ideas of specificity, developmental training, and adaptation, and you must carry it out in a thorough and consistent manner. You may get away with doing some workouts in less than optimal fashion, but to see results you must strive for high-quality training consistency.

Away from the pool, too, you must live your life in a manner consistent with your swim training. This is what is known these days as "hidden training." Remember, rest is a critical part of training. If you're a serious swimmer, you're going to be spending up to 20 percent of your daily life working to improve the swimming capabilities of your body. Consistency demands that you do nothing during the other 80 percent of the time to undermine that positive work.

Alcohol, drugs, and related substances have no place in the life of an athlete. All behavior-modifying substances have been shown to be a long-term detriment to performance. Similarly, any performance-enhancing substances such as anabolic steroids will have extremely harmful long-term effects on your body. Avoid alcohol, steroids, and other drugs. Simply put, as a swimmer you need to live life in a manner that complements your goals, not opposes them.

Now let's look at some examples of training plans for a distance swimmer (800 to 1500 meter), a middle-distance swimmer (200 to 400), and a sprinter (50 to 100) over the course of a 16-week summer season. This will provide a generalized view of training, directed at a high school–age swimmer. To create your own training program incorporating the concepts discussed here, seek the guidance of a professional swimming coach.

4

Sample Workouts

SPRINT WORKOUTS FOR SENIOR SWIMMERS (AGE 15 AND UP)

Sprint training starts by applying principles that are related to all other types of workouts. You begin the season by laying an aerobic foundation with long slow swims. From these you progress to an increasing number of short-rest aerobic sets over the next 3 weeks. During this time you must also do a certain amount of pure (anaerobic) speed work, beginning with 25-yard sprints and progressing, after 4 weeks, to 50s.

During midseason, you should maintain your speed (anaerobic) work by doing a range of sprint distances, from 12½ yards to 25 to 50, and you should also increase the frequency of this pure anaerobic training to three times a week.

The championship season occurs over the final 4 weeks of the season. During this time, your preparation should include a reduction, by about 20 percent a week, in the total distance you swim, with two anaerobic training sessions a week, and a reduction in total anaerobic distance swum in each set. Continue pure speed work on a reduced basis with an emphasis on quality starts and turns.

Below is a sample workout for a senior sprinter in early season training. (All training times relate to a 25-yard pool. On this initial example, I will detail each workout so that you can get a feel for the "shorthand" that is being used.)

133

Long, slow workouts, like the ones these swimmers are performing, help build a strong aerobic foundation.

Early Season

Warmup: Swim easily 600 yards with an emphasis on stroke technique. (Each warmup should have a specific purpose to improve technique. Stroke drills are an excellent warmup device.)

Sets: First, kick 16 × 50 yards (that is, 16 sets of 50 yards each) with a kickboard, working three fast, then one easily. All are done on a 1:10 interval. (In other words, for this exercise you're allowed 1 minute 10 seconds to complete each set; whatever time remains at the completion of a set is used for rest before beginning the next set. In shorthand, 16 × 50 K [kickboard] on 1:10, 3f, 1e.)

Next, swim 5 × 200 pulling with a pull buoy. Swim each one faster than the one before (in swimming parlance, this is known as "descending"), and do each on 2:50. Use alternate breathing. (5 × 200 P on 2:50, buoy, alt. br., descend.)

Next swim 12 × 100 on 1:30, holding a comfortable aerobic pace. Swim these freestyle. (12 × 100 free on 1:30.)

Next swim 8 × 50 free on 1:10, with the first 25 yards and the turn swum fast. (8 × 50 free on 1:10, 1st 25 fast.)

Loosen down: Use a stroke drill for an easy 300 swim.

Midseason

Warmup: 8 × 100 on 1:40 (do 2), then 1:35 (2), then 1:30 (2), then 1:25 (2).

Sets: Do a kick set of 4 × 75 on 1:40, doing the last 25 yards fast.

Then, kick set of 4 × 75 on 1:35, doing the last 50 fast.

Then, kick set of 4 × 75 on 1:30, doing whole 75 fast.

There is no break between the above sets, so it looks like 12 × 75.

Pull a "locomotive" (in swimming, a locomotive consists of swimming laps of increasing distances, each distance in groups of two, the first at an easy pace, usually, the second at a harder pace) up to 4 laps, freestyle, on 30-second intervals (1 lap easy, 1 lap fast, 2 laps easy, 2 laps fast, etc.). The interval is 30 seconds for each lap, so, for example, the 4-lap part of the locomotive is done at a 2-minute rate.

Swim 9 × 100 yards with the first three continuous efforts. Take 3 to 5

Working out with paddles helps increase positive training stress and improves your "feel" for the water.

minutes between swims. These are done very fast. The second three are "broken" at the 50 (stop for :05 seconds and rest at the 50-yard wall).

The last three are broken .05 at each 25-yard wall.

Loosen down: Swim 8 × 100 on 1:45, alternating using the left arm only and the right arm only, with paddles. Swim easily.

Championship Season

Warmup: 400 yards with stroke drills.

Sets: 12 × 50 kick with one done easily, one building up effort, and one fast. The interval is 1:15.

Next pull 5 × 100 free on 1:30, with the last 25 swum strong.

Next, swim 8 × 50 free, with one easy, one fast from a dive start, on 2:00 (the fast ones should be 90 percent of best effort).

Next, swim 8 × 25 free on 1:00, the first four with a fast first 12½, the last four with a fast last 12½.

Loosen down: 400 stroke drill.

MIDDLE-DISTANCE WORKOUTS FOR SENIOR SWIMMERS

If you're a middle-distance swimmer, you should begin the season by building your aerobic base. This aerobic base becomes increasingly important as the distances that you compete in become longer; that is, if you're a 200- to 400-yard or -meter swimmer, you should spend more time building an aerobic base than if you're 50- to 100-yard or -meter sprinter. You can achieve a base by doing long, easy swims and comfortable interval swims and, after the first 3 weeks, some limited speed work. The middle portion of your season should stress aerobic work, with emphasis twice a week on anaerobic training. Your amount of speed work should increase during this period as well.

The championship phase of your season is 3 weeks in length, and sees a 20 percent reduction in mileage per week. You should continue doing aerobic sets but reduce their intensity and duration, and you should also continue

anaerobic sets twice a week but reduce their total volume. You should design
a series of pacework sets to simulate the conditions of a race as well as race pace
effort.

Early Season

Warmup: 600 stroke drill.

Sets: 5 × 200 kick on 4:10, descending.
Pull a ladder (50-100-150-200-150-100-50) with :15 between each distance,
and repeat twice.
12 × 150, with 4 on 2:15, 4 on 2:10, 4 on 2:05, descend 1 to 4 etc. (Descend
1–4 means swim *back one faster.*)
8 × 75, 50, 25, with 75 on 1:10, 50 on 50, 25 on 30. The last 25 of each
swim is fast.

Warmdown: 3 × 200 stroke drill with :30 rest.

Midseason

Warmup: 10 × 100, with 5 on 1:30 and 5 on 1:20.

Sets: Kick with fins: 150 on 2:15, 100 on 1:30, 50 on :45; repeat 3 times.
Swim 4 × 200 on 2:30, descending 1–4
1 × 100 on 1:30
3 × 200 on 2:35, descending
2 × 100 on 1:25   "
2 × 200 on 2:40   "
3 × 100 on 1:20   "
1 × 200 on 2:45   "
4 × 100 on 1:15   "
Pull 6 on 300, 2 on 4:00, 2 on 4:10, 2 on 4:20, second of each pair faster.
10 × 50, 1 easy, 1 fast on 1:00, fast swims holding 200 pace or faster.

Warmdown: 400 warmdown stroke drill.

Championship Season

Warmup: 600 stroke drill.

Sets: 4 × 100 kick with last 25 strong on 2:00.
    4 × 200 pull, buildup, on 3:00. (Buildup means going faster all the way.)
    8 × 100 on 1:45 with 100 easy, 100 pace.

Warmdown: 300 warmdown stroke drill.

DISTANCE WORKOUTS FOR SENIOR SWIMMERS

If you're a distance swimmer, you begin the season with the largest segment of aerobic training compared to sprinters and middle-distance swimmers. You do some speed work for the purpose of retaining your neuromuscular ability to swim fast, but long, slow swimming-over-distance work and easy interval swimming make up the bulk of early season training.

In the middle of your season, you should continue doing aerobic work, but with shorter rest intervals. You should also continue anaerobic work twice per week, plus pure speed work, and your total volume of training should be highest during this middle season period.

The championship phase is the last 3 weeks of the season, and you should reduce your mileage by 20 percent per week, reduce the mileage somewhat in your anaerobic sets, and continue your speed work, with proportionate reduction in the total amount of work.

Early Season

Warmup: 800 stroke drill.

Sets: Kick 200-150-100-50 with :15 rest, repeat twice.
    3 × 500 buildup pulls on 6:30.
    3 × 1000 swims on 1:00 rest, even pace.
    8 × (50 easy/25 fast with 50s on 45, 25s fast on 30).

Warmdown: 400 warmdown stroke drills.

Warmup: 5 × 200, with one free, one 150 free and 50 your stroke, one 100 free/100 stroke; one 50 free/150 stroke, one 200 stroke. Each :30 rest.

Sets: Pull 800 with :40 rest, 600 with :30 rest, 400 with :20 rest. then 200. (Last 200 is strong.)

Set of 3 × 300 on 4:00

3 × 200 on 2:40

3 × 100 on 1:20

2 × 300 on 3:45

2 × 200 on 2:30

2 × 100 on 1:15

1 × 300 on 3:30

1 × 200 on 2:20

1 × 100 on 1:10

Kick 8 × 125, with four on 2:30, four on 2:20.

10 × 50 with the turn and the second 25 swum fast, on :55.

Warmdown: 400 warmdown.

Championship Season

Warmup: 600 stroke drill.

Sets: 5 × 100 kick on 2:10 (25 easy, 50 strong, 25 easy).

3 × 200 on 3:00 with 100 easy, breathing 3, 100 build, breathing 5, 100 easy, breathing 3.

2 × 50 easy on :45, 100 pace on 1:30, repeat 5 times.

Warmdown: 400 stroke drills.

STROKE-SPECIFIC WORKOUTS FOR SENIOR BREASTSTROKERS AND BUTTERFLYERS

All swimmers who specialize in a particular area train primarily with the time-specific groups that they are a part of. A sprint butterflyer trains with the sprinters, a middle-distance backstroker with the middle-distance swimmers, etc. Certain sets are designed to strengthen specific technique needs for each stroke. Even certain workouts may be exclusively devoted to the needs of the specific stroke. How much of a stroke to train is very individualized, and the information below is only a general guide.

In the early season, you should swim 20 to 30 percent of your work in your specialized stroke, in the middle of your season 50 to 60 percent, and an increasing percentage at the end of your season. Much of your aerobic training may be done freestyle.

Also in the early season, you can devote some of your work to long swims in your stroke, and/or to locomotive swims. Maintaining good technique is the primary determinant of how lengthy the long swims should be.

Midseason

Warmup: 600 with first 300 being 75 free, 25 your specialized stroke; second 300 is 50 free, 50 your stroke.

Sets: Kick 50 easy, 25 fast, 50 easy, 50 fast, 50 easy, 75 fast, 50 easy, 100 fast (repeat twice). Repeat base of 30 seconds per 25. All are kicked in your stroke.

Pull 8 × 150, with first four 75 freestyle, 75 your stroke, on 2:15, second four all stroke on 2:20.

Swim 24 × 100, with first eight 6 free, 2 stroke, second eight 4 free, 4 stroke, third eight 2 free, 6 stroke. Swim with a 1:30 base. Emphasis is on the stroke 100s.

10 × 50 on 1:30, 50 easy free, 50 dive (off the starting block), swimming your stroke on the watch (that is, your coach should time you).

Warmdown: 400 stroke drill.

INDIVIDUAL MEDLEY WORKOUTS FOR SENIOR SWIMMERS

Middle-distance training principles apply. Four of your workouts per week should be done only in stroke, but rotating strokes during the week. For example, on Monday morning you should concentrate on freestyle, on Tuesday afternoon the backstroke, on Thursday morning the breaststroke, and on Friday afternoon the butterfly. You should do four workouts per week with stroke-switching as the primary emphasis. You should strive for equal development of all the strokes and not neglect the weakest of them. The very best individual medley swimmers can swim each stroke aggressively during a race if tactics call for that. Such capability is possible only if the swimmer has developed each stroke sufficiently to have confidence in it.

Warmup: 6 × 200, with three reverse IM on 3:00, three regular IM on 2:50.

Sets: 9 × 100 kick, with three butterfly to backstroke on 2:00, three backstroke to breaststroke on 1:55, three breaststroke to freestyle on 1:50.

12 × 250 IM, three going 50 butterfly/backstroke/breaststroke, 100 freestyle on 3:40.

Three going 50 butterfly/backstroke, 100 breaststroke, 50 freestyle on 3:40.

Three going 50 butterfly, 100 backstroke, 50 breaststroke, 50 freestyle on 3:30.

Three going 100 butterfly, 50 backstroke, 50 breaststroke, 50 freestyle on 3:20.

Pull 20 × 75, 10 in weak stroke, on 1:15, 10 in strong stroke on 1:10.

24 × 25, with one easy, 12½ fast, 12½ easy, one fast done 6 of each stroke on :40.

Warmdown: 100 yards each stroke, easy.

TRAINING FOR SWIMMERS AGE 10 AND UNDER

The youngest swimming athletes need especially to develop stroke skills and race techniques, and this should be the major thrust of their training. Wherever possible, age-group training should consist of drills, games, and related learning devices that both mold disciplined learning and training techniques and offer an enjoyable experience. The same general principles of training apply to youngsters, and aerobic development is paramount. In training sessions for very young swimmers, the total amount of time in the water and the amount of energy expended should be limited, so that the swimmers are always eager to do more. Certain types of speed work in quantity should be avoided, since the swimmers' young bodies have not developed sufficient energy chemistry to benefit from it.

Here are two types of workouts for swimmers under the age of 10.

A Learning Workout

Warmup: 12 × 25 freestyle on 50 seconds, with freestyle kick on odd numbers, and one-arm stroke drill alternating left and right arms on the even-number 25s.

Instruction: Learning butterfly with a set of 8 × 50 on lots of rest, with the first 12½ swum complete stroke, the second 12½ kicked, breathing to the front, the next 12½ swum whole stroke, and the first 25 with left arm only on odd-numbered 50s, right arm only on even-numbered 50s.

Instruction: 5 × freestyle start with a sprint for 12½ yards.

Aerobic Training: 6 × 75 on 15 seconds rest, with three each, backstroke, breaststroke, butterfly (the fly should be done left arm, right arm, whole stroke). Repeat twice.

Instruction: Freestyle flip turns. Start in the middle of the pool and do 5 × 50-yard freestyle sets so that each 50 has two turns. Rest between and demonstrate or discuss turns.

Warmdown: 12 × 25 freestyle on 45 with various stroke drills.

An Aerobic Training Workout for Young Swimmers

Warmup: 12 × 25 stroke drills on 45 (do three of each stroke: freestyle, butterfly, breaststroke, backstroke).

Sets: 5 × 200 freestyle on :15 rest. Descend 1 to 3, #4 easy, #5 fast.

Alternate a 25 kick, then a 50 swum on :10 rest, doing all four strokes and repeat 4 times.

12 × 25 butterfly, breathing on every two strokes, concentrating on good timing, on :50.

600 swim: the first 150 is a free stroke drill, the second 150 is backstroke whole stroke, the third 150 is breaststroke stroke drill, and the fourth 150 is freestyle breathing every third stroke.

Warmdown: 10 backstroke turns from 12½ yards out from the wall.

TRAINING FOR SWIMMERS AGES 11 TO 14

In the middle age groups, training should emphasize considerable development of the aerobic capacity, because science tells us that this is the time when the human body is best able to consolidate aerobic gains. Stroke technique, too, is of considerable importance, and should continue to receive high priority. In addition, some speed work can be introduced, and the quality of work can be very high, particularly among girls between the ages of 12 and 14. Introducing a great deal of anaerobic work to exploit the potential for early fast swimming should be avoided, however, since much more substantial rewards can come from the continued development of the aerobic energy system. This is a time when young swimmers should understand the long-term benefits of delayed gratification. For young men, aerobic development generally comes a little later and can be extended with favorable results for a longer period of time. Below are some typical workouts for aerobic development in this age category. One is for swimmers barely out of the younger age groups; the second is considerably more challenging. But both are geared to this age category.

Workout #1

Warmup: 800 with 100 whole stroke, 100 stroke drill.

No matter what type of workout you are doing, always strive for proper stroke mechanics.

Sets: 12 × 50 kick with fins on 1:10

Alternate 5 × 100 freestyle at easy aerobic pace with 5 × 100 stroke at faster aerobic pace, with :20 rest.

Pull 6 × 150 freestyle, breathing every third stroke, on 3:00.

12 × 25 backstroke, breaststroke, and butterfly, alternating stroke drill and whole stroke on :45, emphasizing good technique.

200 freestyle at easy aerobic pace.

10 × 25 free fast on :30.

Warmdown: 400 individual medley, alternating 50 fast, 50 easy.

Workout #2

Warmup: 1000 freestyle; alternate 75 swim buildup with 25 kick

Sets: Kick 5 × 200 with fins, on 3:30

Pull 20 × 75, alternate freestyle and backstroke on 1:20 for freestyle, 1:30 for backstroke.

Swim 5 × 150 freestyle descending 1-5 on 2:30, with easy 50 stroke on 1:10 between the 150s.

Swim 4 × 400 on :15 rest:

#1 - Butterfly, alternating 25 whole, 25 drill
#2 - Backstroke, whole stroke build by 100s
#3 - Breaststroke, whole stroke build by 100s
#4 - Freestyle, alternate breath every 2, 3, 4, 5 by 100s.

Warmdown: 8 × 50 stroke drill freestyle on 1:00.

5

Dry-Land Training

Dry-land training is a useful supplement to actual swim training since it can add strength, power, and flexibility to a swimmer's total development. To a limited degree, it can also aid a swimmer's muscular endurance. There are a variety of types of dry-land training, each with its advantages and disadvantages. In this chapter, we will discuss four types, offer the advantages and disadvantages of each, and suggest a few useful exercises from each category. Any library or bookstore with a good section on athletics or exercise will provide you with entire books covering each of these areas in greater detail.

First, let's look at some general philosophies and considerations for dry-land exercise in coordination with a swimming program.

The primary tenet is that *swimmers need to create strength on land that can be converted later into speed in the water.* An excess of strength beyond that needed to create and maintain speed is "wasted" muscle development. It can even be detrimental to the swimmer, because he or she must carry and "feed" muscle tissue that will never be recruited for swimming faster. In short, muscular development can be overdone.

The second idea is that *it is best to develop strength on land* (because it is easier on land to overload the muscles) *and endurance in the water* (because water training is muscularly and cardiovascularly specific).

Third, it is important for *a trained coach to evaluate any weaknesses that a swimmer may have in dry-land training.* Strength and flexibility training can be tailored rather precisely.

Fourth, it is important to realize *at what age dry-land training can be effective.* Stretching routines, isokinetic work, and tubing work, when properly supervised, can be useful as early as age 8. "Weight work" whether machine or free weights, will not be useful, and may be dangerous, prior to puberty. In

147

You should aim to develop strength on land that can later be converted into speed in the water.

individual cases, it may be better to delay weight training even longer than the onset of puberty.

In all of the discussions to come, one factor should be clearly understood. None of these exercises is useful, and all can be dangerous, if they are done improperly. Whenever possible, all dry-land work should first be demonstrated to the swimmer, and if equipment is involved, all workouts should be supervised. Let's begin by looking at the simplest possible exercise routines: partner exercises with towels.

PARTNER EXERCISES WITH TOWELS

Advantages:

1. The only equipment required is a simple towel.
2. These are excellent exercises for early season preconditioning.
3. They are excellent for young athletes. Very safe.
4. They can be done anytime you have a partner.

Disadvantages:

1. The exercises have only limited application in building muscle size.
2. Improvement in the exercises is difficult to monitor accurately.

Sample Partner Exercises with Towels

1. Shoulder lifts: one partner lifts, the other resists.
2. Curls: one partner does a curl, the other resists.
3. Triceps extension: one partner extends, the other resists.
4. Butterfly lifts: one partner presses hands and arms up and out, the other resists.
5. The basic situp with partner (legs bent).
6. Leg snaps: active partner uses stomach muscles to drive legs toward partner, who pushes them back down.
7. A variety of stretches with a partner. Note that the partner takes no active role, but simply acts as a restraint for the person actively stretching. All stretching is done slowly, with no bouncing motions.

Exercises with a Towel

Shoulder lifts with a partner and a towel.
Holding a towel at chest level, one partner tries to lift his arms while the other partner pulls downward on the towel.

Towel curls.
Holding a towel at waist level, one partner tries to perform arm curls while the other partner pulls downward on the towel.

EXERCISES WITH SURGICAL TUBING

Advantages:

1. They are inexpensive.
2. Young athletes can do them safely.
3. They are good while traveling, can be done anywhere.
4. They are advantagous during the taper phase of one's program, as they can be used to maintain strength that has been built with machines or weights, but without the attendant soreness.
5. The exercises closely simulate the swimming movement.
6. Several of the exercises can closely simulate the hand acceleration during stroke.

Disadvantages:

1. Surgical tubing can be dangerous to work with if the material has deteriorated with age or usage. Equipment supervision is essential, and worn or cracked tubing should be discarded before it becomes a danger.

Sample Surgical Tubing Exercises

1. Triceps extension
2. Biceps curl
3. Shoulder lifts: begin with hands at side and lift.
4. Partner pulls. Careful!
5. Chin lifts
6. Pulldowns

Surgical Tubing in the Water

One recent addition to strength programs for swimming is the use of surgical tubing in the water. The exercises involve hooking one end of the tubing to a belt around the waist of the swimmer, and the other around an object securely attached to the pool itself.

This hookup can then be used in one of two modes, either as a *resistance device* (swimming against the pull of the cord) or as a *speed-assisting device* (swimming with the pull of the cord). Further, it can be used for full stroke work, or to isolate pulling or kicking. Depending upon the length of the tubing used, the swimmer can exercise tethered in place or can swim with it against the tubing's resistance the length of the pool. In addition, surgical tubing is an effective device for all forms of interval or goal swimming. An interesting variation to tethering an in-pool swimmer to a stationary object is to hook two swimmers together in the middle of the pool and have them work in opposition to each other.

Surgical Tubing Exercises

Triceps extension.

Surgical tubing makes an excellent device for a push-through exercise like the triceps extension. However, always make sure that the tubing you use is in good repair. Never perform any exercises with worn or frayed surgical tubing, and be careful when releasing it at the end of an exercise set. For that matter, never release surgical tubing when it is stretched—you could injure yourself or others.

Surgical Tubing Exercises (Cont.)

Biceps curl.
In this exercise, you simply curl the paddles and tubing up to your shoulders.

A

B

C

A

Pulldowns.
By hooking the surgical tubing around a stationary item such as a diving board, exercises that simulate swimming strokes, like the pulldown, can be easily incorporated into the dry-land routine.

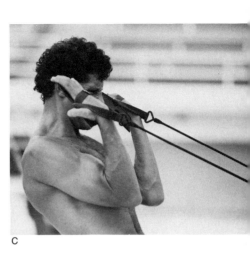

A

B

C

D

Shoulder lifts.
In this exercise, begin with your hands in front of you (A), and lift upward (B, C) until they are even with the vertical plane of your head (D).

B

C

D

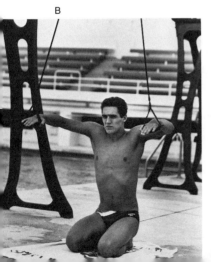

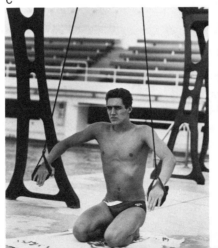

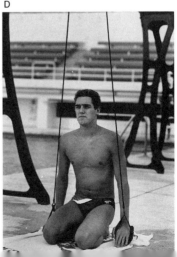

ISOKINETIC EXERCISES (SWIM-BENCH TYPE)

Advantages:

1. They are relatively safe.
2. They are excellent for age-group swimmers.
3. They closely simulate swimming movements.
4. They can be very effective during taper periods.
5. They can help a swimmer develop both strength and speed.
6. They lend themselves to objective analysis and competitive motivation through comparison.

Disadvantages:

1. Isokinetic machines are relatively expensive and require maintenance.

Typical Isokinetic Exercises

All isokinetic work on a swim bench can be done in such a way as to almost exactly duplicate swimming motions. Swimmers usually work the machines for a predetermined time interval or a set number of pulls. The photographs that follow show swimmers using the equipment in a variety of ways to reproduce swimming motions. You can work isokinetic machines at accommodating resistances (the harder you pull, the more the machine resists) and at varying speeds. The more sophisticated isokinetic machines include a computer attachment that measures force generated and total work accomplished in each workout. This data can be useful for motivation and comparison purposes.

Isokinetic exercise machine.
On typical isokinetic exercise machines for swimmers, resistances can be modified, and electronic devices measure the amount of work performed. As shown on the next four pages, such machines allow swimmers to duplicate the four major strokes.

Typical Isokinetic Exercises for Swimmers

Freestyle.

A

B

C

Breaststroke.

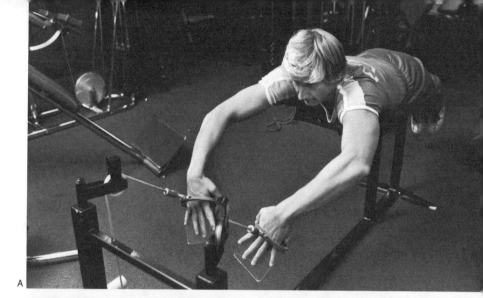

A

B

C

Butterfly.

B

C

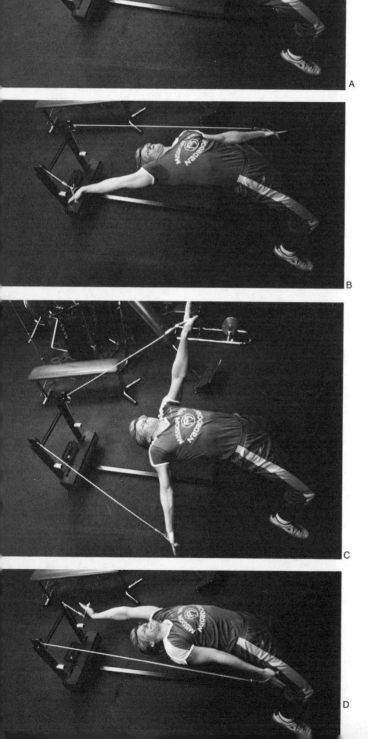

Backstroke.

A

B

C

D

Advantages:

1. Both are safer than free weights while using heavy resistance.
2. They lend themselves to circuit training with large groups.
3. It's easy to evaluate progress on a Nautilus or Universal machine.
4. These machines can help develop large muscle bulk and prime mover muscle strength.
5. They are the safest devices for doing "negative" work, which is very effective for fast strength gains.
6. They can be supervised relatively easily.

Disadvantages:

1. The machines can be dangerous if poorly supervised.
2. Machines are the most expensive way to train with weights.
3. The way machines isolate prime mover muscles fails to develop small supporting muscles. The machine provides stability and support which the body must otherwise provide in actual swimming conditions. In short, if you train strictly with machines you'll discover a lack of development of balance and coordination during exertions, lack of variety in training movements over time, and constrained movement patterns. Don't rely on machines exclusively for your strength gains.

Exercises for Nautilus and Universal Equipment

An exhaustive exploration of the exercises available on machines is beyond the scope of this book. Shown here are some examples of swimmers doing typical exercises with Nautilus or Universal equipment. There is a vast array of exercises possible with both types of equipment, and almost all exercises devised with free weights can be done on the appropriate machine.

Typical Nautilus and Universal Exercises for Swimmers

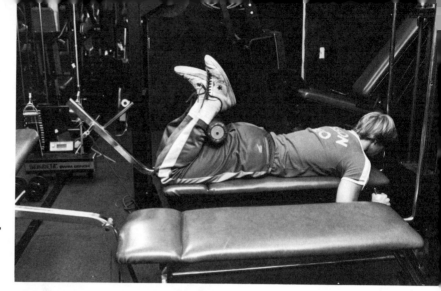

Hamstring curls—
Universal machine.

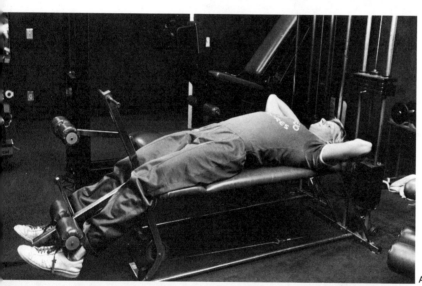

Leg extension exercise—
Universal machine.

A

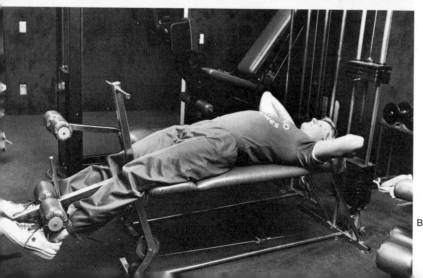

B

A   B

Pull-ups—
Universal machine.

**Chin-ups—
Universal machine.**

**Incline bench press—
Universal machine.**

**Lat pull-downs—
Universal machine.**

**Narrow-grip pull-downs—
Universal machine.**

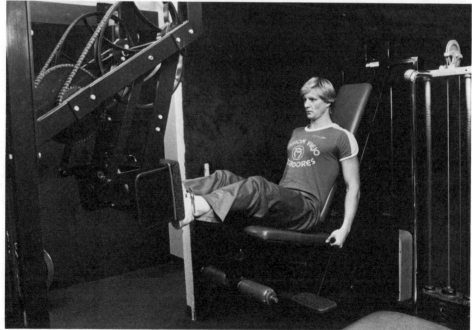

Leg press—Nautilus.

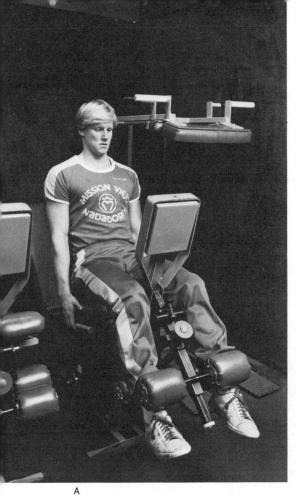

A

Quadriceps lift—Nautilus.

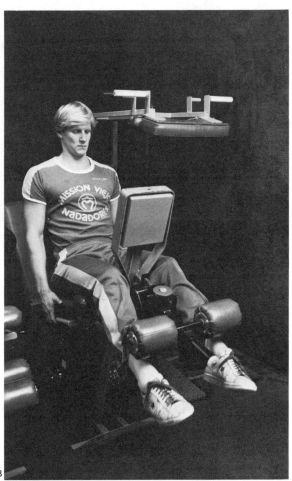

B

A

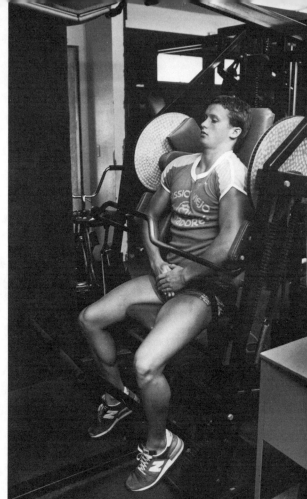

B

Pull-overs—Nautilus.

Pectoral exercise—Nautilus.

A

B

Lat/shoulders push-down exercise—Nautilus.

Forearm pull-over—Nautilus.

Advantages:

1. Traditionally, free weights are the fastest means to build strength.
2. They lend themselves to circuit work with large groups of trainees.
3. They can be done inexpensively, with homemade equipment.
4. They can be used for negative work with fast results.
5. Exercises with free weights can be done at varying speeds.
6. Free weights exercise small muscles as well as large.
7. Free-weight exercises can be done with barbells or dumbbells.

Disadvantages:

1. Free-weight exercising requires the most supervision.
2. Free-weight exercising requires trained personnel to "spot" trainees as well as to supervise.
3. Free-weight exercises can be dangerous to the individual if the exercises are done incorrectly.
4. Free-weight exercising can produce considerable muscle soreness, as can other forms of strength training.

Free-Weight Exercises

The list of free-weight exercises is endless, and a swimming coach is the best judge of those exercises that will be of the most benefit to you. For detailed instructions in various free-weight and machine exercises, see *Sports Illustrated Strength Training: Your Ultimate Weight Conditioning Program,* by John Garhammer, Ph.D. (New York, *Sports Illustrated Winner's Circle Books,* 1987). Free weights are excellent means to correct individual weaknesses and develop specific needs. It's easy to overdo free-weight work, and it's the most stressful form of dry-land training that you can do, so be sure to work only under the guidance of a trained supervisor. (A special note regarding "negative work": This involves exercises where the weight is lifted by one or more spotters, and the subject lowers the weight while controlling it. Negative work can lead to substantial strength gains, but it is also the most dangerous way to lift, since you are working with a weight that you could never handle by yourself. Do negative work *only* under expert supervision.) A final word: Only mature athletes should use free weights, due to the potential danger involved. You coaches out there: Supervise, supervise, supervise!

STRETCHING AND FLEXIBILITY

Flexibility is a key component to swimming success, and it can be enhanced and developed through a planned program of exercises. Flexibility can also be overdone, and injury can result from improper application of stretching work. There are several keys to successful application of stretching and flexibility exercises:

1. When working with a partner, the person being stretched must be in control of the activity at all times. Youngsters working together may sometimes become involved in horseplay and inadvertently overstretch a partner. The person being stretched must communicate with the partner to tell him clearly when to stop a stretch.

2. When stretching individually, avoid bouncing or jarring movements in the stretch. Use slow, steady pressure to increase the range of motion.

3. All stretching should proceed from easy, relaxed movements to the more challenging stretches. Use stretching as a warmup exercise, but practice the same principles of gentle warmup to avoid muscle tears and other injuries.

Advantages:

1. Stretching provides an effective means to increase the range of motion of the joints.

2. Stretching can be performed effectively with groups of athletes.

3. Stretching requires no equipment.

4. Stretching lends itself to circuit training.

5. Stretching can be effective for swimmers of all ages.

Disadvantages:

1. Stretching exercises need to be done properly. Supervision and education are a must!

2. Partner exercises can be dangerous if careful cooperative attention is not offered.

Flexibility Exercises

1. Arm swinging—single and double, used to loosen the shoulder joint, can start slowly and then accelerate to speed.

2. Streamline stretch. Assume the streamline position as if pushing off the wall, and stretch upward.

3. Shoulder stretching, with gentle pressure.

4. Partner shoulder stretching, gently, with communication.
5. Upper back stretch.
7. Horizontal arm swings.
8. Trunk twisting. Start slowly and accelerate.
9. Toe touching.

When developing a stretching and flexibility program, you should consider incorporating stretching into a full routine that would include calisthenics and bodyweight strength exercises such as pushups, situps, etc. These groups of exercises should be done in a set order to warm the body up for practice or competition. Such a routine can be modified for use at any time throughout the season, and it helps the body become attuned to strenuous exercise in a steady, regulated way.

Typical Stretching Exercises for the Competitive Swimmer

Arm swinging.

Streamline stretch.

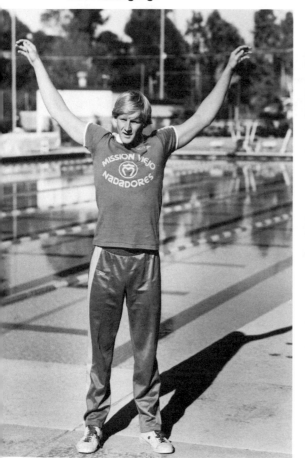

Typical Stretching Exercises (Cont.)

Shoulder stretching with gentle pressure.

Partner shoulder stretches.

Do these gently, with communication.

I.

II.

III.

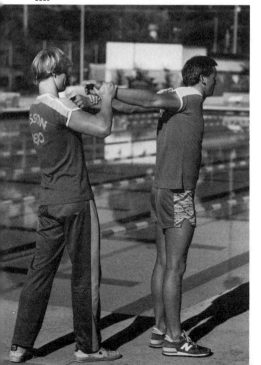

IV.

Upper back stretch.

Horizontal arm swings.

A

B

A

B

Trunk twisting.

Toe touching.

A

B

DESIRABLE COMPETITIVE SWIMMER'S DIET

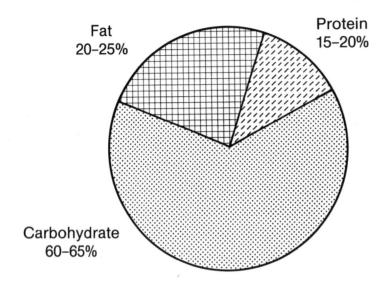

Fat
20–25%

Protein
15–20%

Carbohydrate
60–65%

AVERAGE AMERICAN DIET

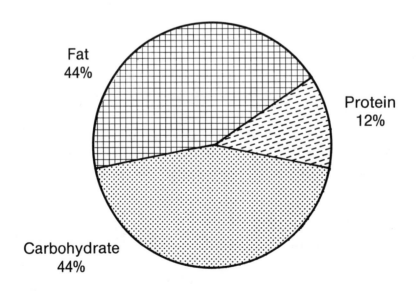

Fat
44%

Protein
12%

Carbohydrate
44%

If you're going to swim competitively, try to limit your intake of fat to 20-25 percent of your total caloric intake.

6

Nutrition

LEARNING HOW TO EAT

For most Americans who have never suffered for want of food, eating is as much an entertaining experience as a nutritional need. Food is a reward, an escape, a high. But in reality, food is a *fuel*. Without the proper food, your body performs poorly. Poor nutrition over an extended time period leads to obesity, sickness, even death.

As a swimming athlete, you must learn what your body needs for fuel and how it uses what you give it. What you feed your body will affect your ability to lose fat or gain muscle. It will affect your energy level, your strength, and your performance in practice and in meets. It will affect your ability to concentrate and to sleep. It will affect your moods.

In the following pages, I hope you will learn in simple, nontechnical terms *how to eat*. There are three major questions to be answered in developing a sound eating program.

1. What kind of food should I eat?
2. How much can I eat?
3. When should I eat?

When you have finished reading this chapter, you will be able to determine your own answers to these questions. You will have an eating plan that will keep you healthy, keep you lean, and keep you swimming fast.

Many of us in this sport know examples of national-caliber swimmers with

178 poor eating habits. Don't follow their example. They are swimming fast in spite of their poor diet *and could be swimming even faster if they were to feed their bodies what they need*. Learning how to eat is as important as learning how to train or learning how to compete. Give yourself the edge. Learn to eat right.

WHAT DO I EAT?

The primary reason why people in general, and athletes in particular, make so many mistakes when it comes to proper nutrition is that so few people really understand what they should eat. If you think about food at all, other than choosing by taste, you probably see food as belonging to four groups: milk products, meats, fruits and vegetables, and grain products. We traditionally think of these groups as equally important. But selecting equally from these categories can leave you eating a high-fat diet, which will negatively affect your performance and your ability to control your weight.

Rather than view food by groups, it's more effective to view them as your body does—broken into component parts. Anything that you put in your mouth to eat will consist of one or more of the following:

1. Carbohydrates
2. Protein
3. Fat
4. Vitamins and minerals
5. Water

Nutritional studies have shown that the best diet for performance, muscle gain, and fat loss should:

1. emphasize carbohydrates,
2. contain adequate protein,
3. minimize fat,
4. include at least a general multivitamin with minerals, and
5. involve drinking considerable amounts of water.

CARBOHYDRATES

Until recently, most people were taught to believe that carbohydrates are fattening. This is not true. Carbohydrates are not fattening. In fact, carbohydrates—complex carbohydrates, that is—are the body's preferred fuel. While your body can use protein and fat for energy, it does so reluctantly, since protein is primarily used to rebuild cells and fat is a stored fuel for emergencies. Using the analogy of a car, it will run on various kinds of gasoline, but will perform best when given the fuel it was designed to run on.

Carbohydrate foods are the highest-energy foods you can eat. They are also the highest-fiber foods you can eat. Because of this second fact, they tend to be relatively low in calories. With similar-size portions of carbohydrate, protein, and fat, you will be eating different amounts of calories. A gram of carbohydrate contains approximately 4 calories, but because carbohydrate foods are generally bulky, they comprise the largest portion relative to fat and protein. A gram of protein contains 4 calories as well, but because of its denser nature, a volume of protein equal to that of carbohydrate doubles the protein's caloric value.

A high-carbohydrate diet, then, will allow you to eat the greatest volume of food without gaining fat weight as well as provide your body with the greatest amount of its preferred fuel.

Complex Carbohydrates

There are two kinds of carbohydrates, simple and complex. These terms refer to the molecular structure of the carbohydrate, which affects the way your body processes the food. Simple carbohydrates have a simpler structure and are assimilated quickly—for nutritional purposes, too quickly—into the bloodstream. Complex carbohydrates have a more complex structure, assimilate more slowly, and are the first-choice food.

Complex carbohydrates generally include vegetables, fruits, and grain products. Examples:

Potatoes: Any kind, but remember that when you fry them, you are adding fat—eat potatoes steamed or baked.

Breads: Whole-grain breads are the best, especially flourless breads. Read labels to minimize fat and sugar (more on sugar in a moment). White breads tend to have fewer vitamins and minerals even when enriched.

Rice: Whole-grain brown rice is preferred to white rice.

Cereals: Whole-grain cereals are nutritionally best. Read labels and avoid sugar.

Noodles (pasta): Whole-grain are best.

Beans: Green beans as well as kidney beans, garbanzo beans (chick-peas), lentils, etc.

Vegetables: Starchy vegetables are preferred to the leafy green.

Still, as we shall see in a moment, it is not enough to eat just a complex carbohydrate diet.

You are choosing among fruits, vegetables, and grain products. If you focus on fruits or on high-fiber vegetables, you will not be eating as effectively as if you focus on starchy vegetables and grain products. Why? A diet high in fruit is also high in sugar. In a moment we'll look at the dangers and drawbacks of sugar to athletic training and performance. Even though fruit sugar (fructose) is not the same as table sugar (sucrose), it is still a simple carbohydrate and will be too quickly assimilated into your body. The primary benefit of fructose as opposed to sucrose is that it will contain more vitamins and minerals in the accompanying fruit. Fruit sugar, honey, and brown sugar are *of themselves* no better for you nutritionally than regular table sugar.

Meanwhile, a diet containing too many high-fiber foods will simply not provide enough calories. As a swimmer, you are using two to three times the number of calories as an ordinary individual. You will need to eat 400 to 600 calories per meal. High-fiber foods such as celery, lettuce, tomatoes, cucumbers—in general the salad vegetables—are primarily cellulose. Cellulose contains calories but is not digestible to the human body. The figures provided by a calorie-counting book are misleading. Use these foods as snacks, but never as the basis for a meal. Nutritional science has shown that if you're an athlete or a person interested in good nutrition, starchy vegetables such as corn, potatoes, peas, and beans, and grains and grain products such as rice, breads, and cereals should make up the bulk of your meals.

Simple Carbohydrates

Simple carbohydrates are better known as sugar. Simple sugars are appetite stimulants, and to some people can be addictive and mood altering; furthermore, they encourage your body to store fat. A gram of sugar has the same number of calories as a gram of vegetable. But sugar is what nutrition scientists call empty calories—it lacks important vitamins and minerals, and because it is an appetite stimulant and potentially addicting, sugar can lead to eating more sugar. Large quantities of sugar can make you fat. But a more important reason for avoiding sugar is the detrimental effect it can have on your performance.

At one time sugar was recommended as a precompetition snack. Because of the simple structure of the sugar, it is immediately assimilated into the bloodstream and provides a burst of energy that you can feel. Your blood sugar level rises rapidly. You feel high on energy. But this is not a normal condition for your body, so it sets about trying to correct the situation. It increases the insulin level in your bloodstream (insulin is necessary for the metabolism of carbohydrates) in order to speed up the removal of the excess blood sugar. Your mechanism for removing sugar is now in overdrive and tends not to shut down at the appropriate time. The result: an energy slump following the energy high. You now experience low blood sugar. You'll feel hungry and tend to want to eat more sugar. But, most important, if you're a swimmer, you will feel tired or physically depressed. You will swim poorly.

Eating sugar can lead to eating more sugar, and you can end up eating too much. Excess calories of any kind are stored as fat. In addition, sugar helps to make your body more efficient at storing fat. Sugar makes you fat when the increase in insulin puts the excess sugar into your fat cells. Sugar also raises your triglyceride level (triglyceride is also fat) and your body stores the excess fat in its fat cells.

Eating sugar can leave you feeling weaker. Muscle development involves cell replacement utilizing amino acids available in the bloodstream. When you eat sugar, protein is used for energy rather than cell building. The presence of sugar in the body essentially blocks protein synthesis. The increase in insulin in response to high blood sugar creates a situation where putting sugar into cells is the primary task. Your body doesn't want to use any fuel other than the sugar to get rid of the overload. Free-floating amino acids (protein) present in the bloodstream are also swept into the cell along with the sugar. It is then used for energy, for activity rather than for cell maintenance or cell development (muscle building). Eventually the muscles weaken.

Examples of foods you should try to avoid if you are serious about competitive swimming: cake, pie, cookies, ice cream, hard candy, chocolate, carob- or yogurt-coated nuts or raisins, frozen yogurt, soft drinks except diet, honey, dried fruit in excess, fruit butters, brown sugar, raw sugar, corn syrup, corn sweetener, molasses, pancake syrup, maple syrup, jams, jellies, doughnuts, canned fruit and fresh fruit in excess, sucrose, fructose, and any foods with any of the above items listed among the first few ingredients.

PROTEIN

Protein-rich foods provide amino acids, the building blocks of your body. Proteins are for building up and maintaining body tissues (such as muscles) during training and growth. If your diet doesn't contain enough protein, your tissue growth will suffer.

Protein deficiency in the American diet is rare. In fact, your diet probably contains more than you need. Often athletes focus on protein consumption at the expense of carbohydrate consumption. When there is not enough carbohydrate in the diet to meet your energy needs, amino acids will be used for fuel. Maintenance and growth of new tissue may suffer. (Note: For muscle growth, carbohydrate consumption is as important as protein. Carbohydrates are needed to fuel the high-intensity weight training used to stimulate muscle growth. Thus, more carbohydrate is needed during weight training to ensure that protein is available for this growth rather than being used for fuel.)

Excess protein, just like excess amounts of other food components, will be stored as fat. Excess protein also results in protein being used for fuel. This amino acid breakdown puts an added strain on your liver and kidneys, which must flush the by-products of the breakdown out of your system. Adequate daily protein intake can be computed at .75 to 1.00 gram per kilogram of body weight. For instance, if you weight 140 pounds (63.5kg), you should consume about 65 grams of protein per day. In general, protein should not exceed 15 to 20 percent of your total caloric intake. If, as a 140-pound swimmer, you require 3250 calories per day (an average requirement for a swimmer), you could eat 122 to 162.5 grams of protein, or nearly 2 to 3 grams of protein per kilogram of body weight. A more effective diet would contain no more than 100 grams of protein, with the remaining calories being spent on carbohydrate. One hundred grams would contain 400 calories and would make up 12 percent of your total calorie intake. The additional 3 to 8 percent can be added to carbohydrate intake to bring that percentage to 78 percent of the total, rather than the usual 60 percent. Unfortunately, most protein foods are also high in fat. To control your fat intake, choose lean sources of protein such as fish, poultry, nonfat dairy products, dry beans, and whole grains. Protein powders also provide a fat-free protein source.

Also, eat protein throughout the day. Your body uses protein for cell building continuously. Be sure you are getting a good-quality protein into your body every 3 or 4 hours. Remember, you do not need to eat meat to be eating protein. Whole-grain breads and other grain products, such as cereals, are excellent sources of protein.

Examples of protein to eat: chicken, turkey, fish (avoid shellfish), lean cuts of beef, nonfat dairy products, beans (all kinds), whole grains, protein shakes.

As an athlete, fat should be cut from your diet to 20 to 25 percent of your total food intake (see the diagram on page 176). Fat-rich foods not only contribute to weight problems (fat gain) but also impede performance. A fat-rich diet results in a "sludgy" oxygen transport system—oxygen is not as effectively carried in the bloodstream. Since swimming, for the most part, is an aerobic activity, oxygen is vital to perfcrmance. If you have a good lung capacity and a strong heart, you are working against yourself with a high-fat diet by slowing down your body's ability to carry oxygen to your muscles. When your muscles run out of oxygen, they "fail." A high-fat diet will have you "failing" sooner than a carbohydrate-rich one.

Restricted oxygen to the muscles also affects your body's ability to utilize fat for fuel. Fat cannot be metabolized without oxygen present. With insufficient oxygen supply, your body turns to its glucose (blood sugar) stores for fuel. If you have not eaten recently, your glucose level will be low and depleted quickly. At that point, your body will use protein (muscle) for fuel. It cannot return to using fat for fuel without slowing down first. At this lower energy expenditure your reduced oxygen need is now being met by the restricted oxygen supply and fat will be burned.

Finally, eating too much fat results in fat gain because fats and oils contain the most concentrated numbers of calories of any foods you can eat. A single gram of fat contains 9 calories—over twice as many as a gram of protein or carbohydrate. These are concentrated calories. A little goes a long way.

Examples of fatty foods to try to limit or avoid: butter, margarine, oil- or cheese-based salad dressings, all vegetable oils, all cooking fats, anything fried, sour cream, cheese, and all other dairy items except nonfat products, eggs, peanut butter, olives, avocados, sauces and gravies, ice cream, nuts, seeds, hot dogs and most lunch meat, bacon, sausage, shellfish, all except the leanest cuts of red meat, and of course, mayonnaise. Note: Try to avoid all types of fat. The issue of animal fat vs. vegetable oil, or saturated vs. unsaturated fat, relates to the subject of cholesterol levels and heart disease. All fats are equally fattening and equally impede performance.

VITAMINS AND MINERALS

After eating a proper diet and following an effective exercise program, taking a high-quality vitamin-mineral supplement is the next most important priority on your health and performance list. To maximize your energy and your performance, it's wise to ensure that you are getting all the essential vitamins and minerals, especially those depleted by stress and exercise, the B-complex vitamins and vitamin C.

WEIGHT LOSS AND WEIGHT GAIN

What if you have a weight problem? How do you solve it? Whether you need to lose or gain weight, strict adherence to a regular schedule of training, eating, and sleep will result in movement toward your target weight.

Weight Loss vs. Fat Loss

Remember that fat loss does not mean weight loss. Always use body composition testing or the fit of your clothes to assess progress in a fat loss program. Do not use a regular scale. Scale weighings can be frustrating and demoralizing. Avoid them.

To focus on body fat reduction while maintaining high performance levels, you should reduce your calorie intake by about 500 calories per day. A reduction of more than 1000 calories per day will cause your performance to suffer, will lead to excessive muscle loss, and will slow down your fat loss. If you need 3250 calories per day, eat 2500 to 2750 calories spread across five or six equal meals. Calorie counting can be tedious. If you are eating a diet high in complex carbohydrates, with very little fat and no sugar, you will not have to count calories.

Body Composition

Athletes should use a measure of body composition to assess the effectiveness of their eating and training program on their muscle and fat content. The composition test tells you what your body is composed of. It breaks down your total weight into two parts: your total lean weight and your total fat weight. It therefore enables you to measure muscle changes independent of changes in your fat. Since you are exercising and watching what you eat, you should expect strength and muscle increases as well as fat losses. What happens to your total weight will depend on how these two changes offset each other. You could lose weight if your fat loss exceeds your muscle gain. You could maintain your present weight if your fat loss exceeds your muscle by a proportionate amount. You could maintain your present weight if muscle and fat changes are equal.

Or you could gain weight if your muscle increases are greater than your fat loss.

You should not necessarily consider weight loss an important goal. It is not a measure of success. It should not be used as a criterion for competing. In general, swimmers are both young and involved in a tremendous amount of exercise. Even without lifting weights, muscles are being stimulated to grow through the work done in the water. At this age, the swimmer is in the midst of a high growth rate. This, coupled with exercise, creates a situation where rapid lean body mass growth occurs. In other words, if you're a young swimmer, you should expect a certain amount of weight gain. If you are eating properly, you can assume that these weight increases are positive—they represent bone and muscle growth. Even if you obviously have weight to lose, do not expect dramatic weight loss. Your continuing muscle gains will offset your fat losses to slow down your total weight loss.

Body Composition Testing

There are several methods for measuring body composition. The most accurate for measuring overall body composition is hydrostatic, or underwater, weighing. Hydrostatic weighing involves submerging the person being tested underwater for short periods of time to determine total underwater body weight. Underwater weight measures are combined with dry-land weight measures, vital capacity measures, and other factors to determine body density. This number is then converted to body composition and body fat percentage. You may find this technique available at a local hospital or health club. Many colleges also provide hydrostatic weighing for their athletes.

Three other measures of body composition are:

1. Anthromorphic measures
2. Skinfold measures
3. Bioimpedence measures

Anthromorphic measures take circumference measures of different parts of the body. Charts and formulas are then used to calculate body composition. This is probably the least expensive form of testing, requiring little more than a tape measure.

Skinfold testing measures folds of skin with a caliper at various locations on the body. These measures are then plugged into formulas to calculate body fat percentages. Costs of calipers range from $5 to $200.

Bioimpedence testing measures electrical current passed through the body.

Since the current is impeded more by fat than by muscle, the speed of flow can be converted into a measurement of body composition. This equipment is very expensive.

Measurement Error

The likelihood of error in techniques other than hydrostatic weighing makes them useless for measuring progress in swimmers' training programs on a month-to-month basis. Measurements of short-term changes in muscle and fat by these methods are suspect. Fat is carried both intermuscularly and under the skin. Depending on how a swimmer carries fat and where measurements are taken, body composition and muscle and fat changes can be over- or underestimated. Fat distribution generally follows gender-related rules, but still is different for each individual. Measuring thigh or buttock circumference, for instance, may adequately capture changes in fat for female swimmers, but not for males, since they tend to carry fat in other locations. Modifying anthropomorphic and skinfold measures to account for these variables can make them useful tools when underwater weighing is not available.

Measuring Progress

Regular body composition testing provides an excellent monitor of training progress. You can determine your ideal body weight and measure progress toward it. The body composition test gives you body fat composition. Do not rely solely on this number. It is used to convert your total weight into fat weight and lean weight measures. Use these numbers for comparison purposes with new figures on a monthly basis. The absolute percentage should not be used as a comparison between swimmers. There are genetic differences in essential fat levels that allow a swimmer with 12 percent body fat to be in as good shape as a swimmer with 9 percent. Use the measurements solely to gauge your own progress.

Target Body Weight

Ideal weight is based on your total lean weight and your ideal fat percentage. There is no one ideal weight for you. As you grow and gain lean weight, your ideal weight will change. You can calculate your ideal weight by taking your total lean weight and dividing it by 1 minus your target fat composition. If your ideal fat percentage is 12 percent (1−12 percent =.88) and your total lean weight is 142.12 pounds, your total ideal weight would be 160.36. At this weight, assuming that you had not lost any lean weight in reaching this goal, your body-fat weight would be 12 percent.

Determining the Target Lean Weight

If you are just beginning swimming, eat poorly, or have not yet developed your musculature fully, you may be undermuscled. In determining your target ideal weight, you should try to increase your target lean weight to a more reasonable number before determining your target ideal weight. For instance, female swimmers may weigh less than 100 pounds and yet have too much fat. You would not set a goal to lose weight, but set one to reach a correct fat percentage. You would show a target increase in lean weight.

Ideal Fat Percentage

The ideal fat percentage in men is 15 percent and in women 22 percent. This is optimum for health. Athletes, swimmers included, tend to carry less fat to increase their strength-to-weight ratio. Male swimmers' fat percentages range from 6 to 12 percent and female swimmers from 12 to 18 percent. The fat percentage for a world-class swimmer (male) is 12 percent. The female counterpart is 19 percent. These can be considered reasonable target percentages. If you are lower than these already, maintain your current level. Track your performance and your fat percentage to determine at what fat level you perform best. Essential fat for men is considered to be 3 to 6 percent (10 to 12 percent for women). At these low levels, your body function is very marginal and performance will suffer. In essence, it is impossible to go "all out" because your body has no reserves. It is not true that swimmers need more fat than other athletes. If you were constantly swimming in cold water, this might be true, but in general, fat impedes muscle performance.

In fact, swimmers often have weight problems because of the tremendous amount of training they do coupled with poor eating habits. Excess stress of any kind contributes to fat accumulation. Overtraining is a situation where the body tends to accumulate fat and lose muscle. This is the exact opposite of what the swimmer is trying to achieve. Such potential problems make it imperative that the swimmer eat right and gain enough rest to handle the stress of training; otherwise, muscle loss and fat gain will occur.

Remember, fat is a storage for emergency. The depletion of blood sugar during training causes hunger. You will generally eat more than your body actually needs in satisfying this hunger, thereby increasing your fat stores.

LEARNING HOW TO
CONTROL YOUR WEIGHT

It is important to understand the concept of weight control. If you are

1. choosing the correct foods,
2. eating the right amount of food, and
3. eating at the right times,

you will be in control of your weight. This is not to say that you will necessarily gain or lose weight. Total weight is not an effective measure of weight control.

Eat before your workout. To maximize performance and preserve muscles, eat before any exercise. If you find that eating makes you uncomfortable, eat primarily complex carbohydrates and eat 15 to 20 minutes before the workout. You will find that as your body becomes accustomed to having food before your workout, it will become more efficient at providing the enzymes to digest it more effectively. If you always eat at the same time, your body will begin digestive processes before you begin eating, in anticipation of the food. Liquid carbohydrate drinks are also available and easily assimilated.

Emphasize many small meals throughout the day. When you skip meals and go for long periods of time without food, your performance will suffer and you make it easier for your body to store fat. Carbohydrate is the first choice of fuel food for performance. If you haven't eaten for some time, your glucose stores will be low, having been used up and not replenished. When you perform, you will be forced to use fat or protein for fuel. In both cases, your muscles do not function as well, and in this case you create a plateau in your performance.

To build muscle, you must train on a regular and consistent basis. You also have to provide adequate carbohydrate to maintain glucose levels, and adequate protein to rebuild muscle on a regular schedule. Eat complex carbohydrates every few hours, and eat protein throughout the day. Carbohydrate is digested and gone within 20 minutes to 2 hours.

The more you deprive your body of food by skipping meals, the more efficient your body becomes at storing fat and other sources of fuel. Your metabolism slows down to accommodate a smaller and smaller food intake. Your digestive system becomes more efficient at extracting all the calories out of the food you give it. When you do eat, your body quickly stores all food as fat. When it is again deprived, it turns to its muscles as well as its fat stores to make up the deficit. It uses muscle because it is guarding fat stores for future use. While your body does not really "think" what it is doing, it has a strong survival mechanism which reacts to "starvation" by implementing systems to protect itself. It uses muscle for fuel. It slows down its metabolism. It stores fat more easily and effectively.

WHEN SHOULD I EAT?

The timing of your eating is the single most important factor in eating effectively. You must follow an eating schedule. Plan your meals so that you are eating every few hours. Make sure that you eat before your workouts, even if you must get up substantially earlier. All meals should be equal in calorie size and balance, unless your practice schedule forces you to eat late at night. Late meals should always be minimized. Adjust by increasing your intake earlier in the day. If you provide your body with enough fuel when it needs it, before workouts, you will be less hungry later. Eat five or six meals during the day, dividing your total calorie requirement equally across the meals. Schedule your meals and do not eat at any other time. Finally, remember that the "how much" question becomes "how much of what, when?"

7

Mental Preparation for Performance

In looking back on the history of sport, it is surprising how long athletes and coaches have been saying that the sports they participate in are "90 percent mental," or "50 percent mental," or whatever the percentage may be. Experts generally agree that the mental side of sports does play a significant role in both training and competition, regardless of the exact percentage. It's possible that the more elite the competition becomes, and the finer-tuned the athletes are physically, the more the difference in performance between athletes becomes a mental difference.

On the other side of the coin, perhaps the most important time to develop mental skills and abilities is as a developing athlete. After all, the elite athlete has found effective strategies by hook or crook to help him succeed. As in many other skills, a few well-learned and steadily practiced techniques form the basic framework for effective mental preparation. We're going to look at those here.

There are really two sides to the discussion of mental preparation, and they are both important to success. The first, which we do not have space here to discuss in meaningful detail, is the idea of developing life skills. These include such things as goal setting, both long and short term, personal organization, and, most important, the concept of self-image formation and change. There are many excellent books on the market that can help swimmers in these areas, and some of the best are listed in the Resources section. I urge you to make use of them. The second side, a more immediate proposition, is the idea of mental preparation for peak performance. The purpose of this chapter is to help you formulate a plan of action so that you can effectively prepare to do your best possible swim on any given day. We will look at three crucial mental skills and describe how they work together to create a peak performance. We'll also describe the process of putting it all together on race day, along with some

191

Any swimming expert will tell you that mental preparation is a chief component of peak swimming performance.

mental gambits for you to try with yourself, and some dangers to beware of. One critical fact that you must grasp as an athlete is that you attain the effective use of mental skills in the same way that you learn to swim a good butterfly stroke. That is, you must exercise the appropriate muscles in the appropriate ways! In this case, constant proper mental practice produces positive results.

One great advantage in the quest to become a mentally prepared athlete that you do not enjoy in learning the butterfly stroke is that the skills you will learn in this chapter can be practiced anywhere, with any subject, at any time. In fact, they will help you in school, in social situations, and in literally every phase of your life. By practicing them in these settings, you will not only gain useful skills for swimming, but you will learn to lead a more effective and satisfying life. You cannot exercise your swimming muscles at all hours and settings, but your mental training need never stop!

Dedicate yourself to learning these skills well, so you can attain the mental advantage so important to success in swimming workouts and competitions as well as in life itself. If you practice these skills conscientiously, this attainment, I promise you, will be one of the most rewarding and satisfying benefits of your swimming career.

OVERVIEW

The first question we need to answer is, "Mental preparation for what?" The answer is, "Mental preparation for a peak performance." A peak performance is defined as that which is the very best the individual is capable of *at that time* (that last phrase is very important). A good swimmer wants to get the very best possible result out of his physical self at any particular moment in the season. His best in the midseason may not be as good as his best later on, but it is the best *at that time,* and should be judged a peak performance.

At another, deeper level, there is a magical feeling that accompanies the peak performance that is, of itself, extremely rewarding. The feeling is common to all sports. The baseball player suddenly goes on a "hot streak" and says he is "seeing the ball real well." Michael Jordan has one of his fabulous games and says he was playing "in the zone." The runner feels that he is floating, running without effort, just barely touching the ground. The swimmer finds everything so easy to do, so simple to execute. All serious athletes have experienced the feeling when "everything just seems to go right." *That* is a peak performance and the feeling is so exciting that if you asked any athlete, he would tell you that he would like to have it whenever possible. Well, it so happens it *is* possible to experience the magical feeling of a peak experience to greater and lesser extents at any time by following the simple processes we will describe.

A simple exercise to begin with will give you an idea of the feeling. Think for just a second of the best swim you've ever had, and try to re-create or feel it in your mind. Describe it in words to yourself.

Chances are excellent that some of the following words or phrases are in your description: "Easy, relaxed, smooth, confident, I could go on forever . . . like I was the only one there, strong, fast, I could see everything so clearly . . . Time slowed down [or speeded up], and I had all the time in the world to do things, I was always moving faster and sooner than everyone else. . . . It was like a dream, it was like I was watching myself perform, I had lots of air, I never got tired . . . I can't remember the actual race, at the end I wasn't tired at all, and . . . I was so happy!"

The point is that there are certain key elements in experiencing a peak performance that are common to most people, and you can direct your mind and body to create the necessary climate for their realization. Your goal, then, is to be able to control and command this remarkable process at your will.

There is a very basic fact that must be recognized when performing a physical skill. That is that an athlete gives his very best performance at times when the physical skill is under the guidance of his subconscious mind. In other words, he performs the skill "on automatic." If basketball players had to think through the motions of a pass or a foul shot, the game could never be well played or exciting. Put simply, *our conscious mind cannot operate fast enough to perform a physical skill effectively.* When we first learn skills, we must "think our way through them." Intuitively though, we know we must learn them to the point of becoming "automatic." At that point, we become skilled athletes.

Our first goal, then, is to put the learned skill, be it as simple as one breaststroke pull or as complicated as a complete 200-meter breaststroke swim, into our subconscious for storage and use at another time.

All of the phrases we used earlier to describe the "magical feeling" relate to a mental state where this use of the subconscious mind has come into play. Indeed, all the phrases relate to some simple facts of physiology that must be present for peak usage of our physical powers.

Science tells us that for peak physical performance our muscles must be warm, relaxed, and literally "loose," which means that the fluid between the muscle fibers must be moving smoothly and easily. We must also have a degree

194 of muscle tension present. The absolute absence of muscular tension is not productive, while an exaggerated degree of tension makes it impossible to perform skillful limb movements. There is a degree of desirable muscular tension, then, that we might describe as the muscular "readiness" that is optimum for good performance. The muscles must be in a ready but simultaneously relaxed state to perform—not limp, not tight, but *relaxed.* Thus, the first element of peak performance that we must learn is muscular *relaxation.* We will learn more about this skill in the next section.

Other things happen in the peak performance state that can be described as changes in time evaluation, or space, or vision recognition. We seem to see things speed up, or more usually slow down, or we see them more clearly. We seem to be in a "focused" state, where only the object that we are responding to attracts our attention. These responses are a by-product of the state of *concentration,* and this is the second major area of skill development in peak performance.

Finally, we do seem to be on "automatic pilot" when we are having a peak performance. We do not have to make any conscious decisions, nor do we have to think about doing something; we just do it. It is as if we are responding to a pre-set script. In fact, that is exactly what we are doing; the script exists in our subconscious, and we activate it as we begin the activity. This script is called a *visualization,* and it is the third vital element in peak performance. We will spend considerable time working on a plan to develop a visualization later in this chapter.

Together, *relaxation, concentration,* and *visualization* make up the "peak performance process." This chapter will teach you the skills necessary to develop each area. There are two applications to the processes we will explain here. First, the skills should be developed on a long-term basis, over a period of months before the key event, or events, of the season. They can also be practiced daily, on a very short-term basis, but *they must be worked on and developed together.* In the second application, the peak performance process has a "short-term trigger" that will help you settle yourself into the proper frame of mental skills directly before an event. This short-term trigger can effectively be used, and is used by many athletes, swimmers included, in as little as 10 seconds. Both short- and long-term applications of the peak performance process will result in very beneficial results for you. The instructions you will receive in this chapter need to be followed correctly and completely, and you must practice these skills daily if you are to see improvement in your swimming and your life.

The term *relaxation* must be thoroughly understood as it relates to the peak performance process. When you are ready to compete, it is important that your muscles have some small degree of tension in them and are not limp. This muscular readiness is necessary for the muscles to exert force to their optimum ability. During the long-term process of preparation for peak performance, you must learn to control and regulate the degree of muscular tension that is present in your body, and in each of the major muscle groups.

Relaxation itself has two major components. The first of these is the commonly understood relaxation of the prime mover muscles that we use when we swim. Equally important, however, is relaxed control of the muscles associated with the breathing mechanism. One of the most common characteristics of a peak athletic performance experience is the feeling of being able to breathe easily and having complete control over that process. At no point is the person gasping for air or having that choking feeling associated with a lack of air. In fact, the expression "to choke" in the clutch is very apt, because the athlete experiencing this momentary feeling of stress has quite literally lost control of the normal breathing process due to an excess of muscular contraction at inappropriate times. One can literally feel a tightness in the throat. Learning to control the breathing process to make it free and easy is a vital concern in the relaxation phase of mental preparation.

Muscular Relaxation Techniques

To develop the degree of muscular and breathing control that you need for a peak performance, you must develop an awareness of muscular tension. To do this, you need to contrast muscular tension in yourself with muscular relaxation. How to do this? Here is one simple method you can use.

It will be helpful if you think of muscular tension as a fluid, such as water, that can flow from place to place. What you are going to do is to learn how to control that flow. You will concentrate on isolated muscle groups and individual muscles, and contrast tension with relaxation to make yourself aware of the presence and absence of tension. First, select a word that you will use as a "trigger" to set the tension into a flow. For our purposes now, let's use the command "Let go." Whenever we say "Let go," we will think of the tension releasing its flow from that muscle. It will be helpful if we think of tension literally "flowing" out of the muscle.

Now, lie down on a comfortable surface. A rug, the grass, or better yet, your bed at night will do just fine. Try to feel and sense your weight on the surface, and be aware of all the places where your body touches the surface. Now, concentrate on your right foot. Suddenly tense it and count "One, two, three, four, five . . . Let go." As you say "Let go," feel and think about the tension flowing, like water, into the surface you are lying on. Use "Let go" as your trigger to release the tension from the muscle. Repeat this several times.

Next, move to the major muscle in the calf of your leg, and tense it and your right foot together. Use the count and the "Let go" mechanism to build and then release tension. Repeat. Then, move up your leg to all its major muscles and alternate tension with the "Let go" release technique to put your leg muscles in a relaxed but ready state.

Continue this process to relax your entire body. Be sure, at a variety of points, to put the entire lower body, or upper body, or left or right side, together. It will be helpful to apply the "Let go" technique to the whole body at some point in the process.

This alternation of tension and relaxation provides your mind and body with an appreciation of the difference between the two states, and becomes a way for you to bring your muscles to the appropriate state of readiness.

Each time you go through a process of mental preparation, you must, to some degree, do the relaxation exercises above. This becomes a preparation ritual that will help greatly in implementing the entire peak process. You should always include this step, even if you feel that you are already relaxed. Hidden tension is a very destructive force when you are seeking peak performance. You also need to develop your personal word or phrase like "Let go" so that your mind and body always associate it with muscular relaxation. This will be of particular importance to you when you use the process in its short form just before an event.

So, you should begin each mental preparation practice with the "Let go" muscular relaxation technique. This will take anywhere from 2 to 10 minutes, depending on the completeness of your efforts. Once you've relaxed your muscles, you're ready to begin work on relaxing your breathing, or "breathing easy."

First, however, there are two muscle groups that you should give some extra attention. The first of these is the muscles of the buttocks. These are large muscle groups, and perhaps social conditioning causes us to overlook the fact

Smart swimmers know that relaxing themselves before a competition helps improve their performance.

that they are important in sports performance of all kinds. You must learn to subject them to the same tension/relaxation exercises as the rest of the body, since much internal tension can be found in these often-overlooked muscle groups.

The second, and probably even more important, muscles are those of the facial group. Humans have a huge number of facial muscles, and these are an accurate reflection of a person's mental state. Look closely at certain swimmers before an event and you literally see the tension in their faces. Observe the faces of people in a race. Those swimming fast and in front are generally relaxed, serene, their faces either masklike or sometimes positively, happily excited. Most, however, are usually placid, with a marked absence of tension. Now contrast these with the faces of those who are not swimming well. These faces will almost always be contorted and tense. The faces show the strain, and as we shall soon see, actually contribute to the strain of the swim.

As an experiment, tighten your face with tension and create, in effect, an "ugly mask." Now try to talk, and notice your breathing as you hold this tense facial expression. Note that your breathing becomes strained, and the tension creeps into your neck, and eventually down into your shoulders and arms in much less time than even the 2 minutes required to swim a 200-meter race. Think how a tense face affects you when you try to compete!

In contrast, now put your face through the relaxation and "Let go" exercises and notice what happens to your breathing! It should be considerably easier, and the tension should have stopped flowing to the rest of the upper body. Controlling the facial muscles is a major skill that you should learn and practice.

Now let's learn some exercises that will help you to develop the skills for "breathing easy."

Relaxing Your Breathing

In addition to muscular relaxation, it is also important to have close control of your breathing muscles. First, let's remember how the breathing mechanism works. A person breathes in when the air pressure inside the lungs is less than that outside the body. This difference is developed in two ways: first, the diaphragm, a sheet of muscles across the body just below the lungs and rib cage, can be raised or lowered. As it is lowered, the total volume inside the rib cage expands and there is room for more air within the lungs. Second, the chest may rise, muscularly, which also increases the volume of the chest cavity, resulting in room for even more air in the lungs. Chemical changes within the lungs, as the composition of the internal air changes, cause these two types of muscular actions to occur automatically. Normal breathing for a relaxed person involves the automatic lowering of the diaphragm. During relaxed breathing, the stomach area moves outward. If you observe a sleeping person, you will see this phenomenon. It's the most relaxed type of breathing, and we call it "belly breathing." When we are stressed, or need great volumes of oxygen, we tend to lift our chest to breathe. This takes substantially more muscular effort and energy than belly breathing. The more we exert ourselves, the more we tend to use every type of mechanism at our disposal to increase the volume of our chest.

As we have already seen, muscular tension is very bad for quality performance. So too is tension or undue exertion in the breathing muscles. Quite literally, a tense face leads to a tense neck, which in turn makes the throat muscles constrict and makes breathing difficult.

In order to control our breathing properly and "breathe easy," we use a method similar to the "Let go" technique we used to relax our muscles. In essence, it involves three types of breathing. To develop your breath control, start by lying down, and after going through the "Let go" muscular-relaxation procedure, lie quite still and try what relaxation specialists call "hidden breathing." That is, try to take in air without appearing to do so. Breathe, in other words, with no muscular movement. Next, breathe more deeply; do "chest breathing" by lifting your chest and inhaling and exhaling deeply. Then do a "dragon's breath" by breathing as deeply and as quickly as possible, expending a great deal of effort and energy to get the air in and out. (Warning: Do this for only a few breaths, as it is quite possible to hyperventilate and momentarily lose consciousness if you use this technique for more than a few seconds.) After a few "dragon breaths," relax into belly breathing, and concentrate on feeling the difference. Continue to belly breathe while saying to yourself the phrase "Breathe easy." As you'll discover, it's possible to begin to feel a great sense of overall muscular relaxation once your breathing process is under control. The purpose of the exercise is to contrast the ways in which we breathe. This awareness of our breathing processes allows us to effectively control our breathing patterns. Research has found that belly breathing is the optimum breathing state to be in when we begin a competition.

Now remember the key words that you will use every time in your muscular relaxation process: "Let go" and "Breathe easy." In one sense, there is nothing magic about these words, and you should feel free to select any that mean the same thing to you, but *there is magic in the process.* By having real control over your muscles and breath, you have taken a substantial step in the peak performance process.

CONCENTRATION

It has been said that concentration is the greatest art of all, and that without concentration, there would be no art. Certainly successful people in all walks of life, and in all endeavors, will list the ability to concentrate among the most important ingredients in their success.

Despite its importance, however, concentration is not an easy thing to define. To a certain extent, we can define it by what it is not. It is not meditation, where one empties one's mind. On the contrary, one fills one's mind in concentration. All the great religions and philosophies in the world have ways to describe it or think about it. For the purposes of this discussion, it will be helpful to think of concentration as the ability to focus attention. Attention, literally, is the state of attending, or applying the mind, to something.

Two models of concentration are very useful. One is a sending model, and one is a receiving model. We must concentrate to send messages from our mind to other parts of our body, and we must equally concentrate to receive messages from the world around us. Both of these models relate directly to swimming, as we shall see.

The sending model is rather simple. Imagine a light bulb on a lamp sitting on a table in a dark room. When the light bulb is turned on, the light fills the room. It is evenly spread throughout the room, and is not terribly bright and intense in any one part of it. Now imagine taking a white piece of cardboard and standing it on one side of the bulb. The opposite side of the room now receives almost all of the light from the bulb. Only half of the room receives light, and it is a more intense, penetrating light. If we were to gradually make a funnel of the cardboard, we would reduce the area that the light can shine on. As we do that, the light is intensified on that gradually diminishing area and the rest of the room grows darker. We have *concentrated* the light. We have done this by restricting the area that the light can shine on. That is our example of a sending model. Similarly, we can concentrate the "light" of our minds to "shine" (send signals) to any part of our body that we choose.

The receiving model is slightly more complex. Imagine a TV station with a large number of receiving antennas on top of the hill behind it. Each is pointed in a different direction and therefore receives different signals. The information being received in the station is varied and diverse. Gradually we turn half the receivers in the direction of one signal. That will mean that we receive that signal much more strongly than any of the others. As we turn more and more receivers in that direction, we receive more and more from that signal, and less and less from any other. We are *concentrating* our ability to receive information by eliminating the attention we are paying to other signals.

Both models are easy to apply in swimming. In sending messages to different parts of our body, we might need to concentrate, say, on our elbow in the 1650 freestyle event if we tend to drop it late in the race. We need to pay close attention to that aspect of our stroke, and think about that elbow and its position. In the receiving mode, we listen, for example, only for the starter at the beginning of the race, ignoring all distractions around us. During a race we might listen only for our coach's voice. The roles that these two models play in fulfilling our racing needs are many, and we will explore more of them as we continue. The question now is, How do we exercise our ability to concentrate in the peak performance process?

Concentrating During the Peak Performance Process

One of the things we know about concentration is that in order to concentrate, we must have something to concentrate on. It is impossible to concentrate on nothing. In most situations, our minds will fill themselves with something. What we want to be able to do is choose the appropriate object of concentration and learn to enhance our ability to keep our attention on it.

To prove this to yourself, try to concentrate on something like a blank white piece of paper. See how long you can devote your whole attention to it. Now try it with the comics page of the newspaper. Chances are, most of you will have a much easier time keeping your mind on the cartoons than on the blank page. Why? Because there is more there to *occupy* your mind. There is color, story, figures, dialogue, and humor. This is worth noting as we develop our ability to concentrate. *The more complex the object of concentration, the easier it is to concentrate on it.*

In swimming, we have the perfect object for our concentration, and that is the water. Water is extremely complex. Think of all the things about it you can concentrate on: its color, temperature, smoothness, motion, sound, texture, smell, and all the combinations thereof. Water is not only complex, it is extremely attractive to humans. People everywhere are attracted to live, work, play, look at, or just be near the water. Water is a perfect object of our concentration, and it is the medium in which we perform as swimmers.

Following your muscular relaxation and breath control periods, you should try to lead your mind into a concentrated state. To do this, begin by picturing the water in your pool, or in a pool you will soon swim in. Examine it mentally, and go through all of its properties. Mentally see, hear, feel, smell, and taste it. You can also do this at the pool, before practice or before a meet. What you are trying to develop is your ability to concentrate on one thing at a time. As you concentrate, develop a key word, "water," that you associate with the state of concentration. As with the relaxation phrases, you will use this key word frequently.

Now, everyone has greater or lesser success in concentrating. What should you do when the mind wanders? Simple. Bring it back. Restart the process. Another way of coping with a wandering mind during concentration practice is to restate and refeel all the properties of the water. Remember, the way to increase concentration is to delve more deeply into the subject. The more intricate the object, the easier it is to concentrate. By focusing attention on one thing, we remove all the distractions in the environment around us.

Let's now look at some specific situations where good concentration can help your swimming. The first is when you go to your first big meet—the first meet at any level is a major new experience in your life. Your purpose in coming to the meet is to swim fast. Yet all around you are new people, new surroundings, new procedures. At the national swimming level you may find yourself next to famous swimmers and coaches whom you have read about or seen on TV. It's extremely easy to lose your concentration. You must instead *force your mind to focus on your purpose for attending the meet, and on what you must do to achieve your goals.* Practicing concentration with the use of a concentration device, be it "water," or "winning," or "fast," or some other key word.

A second example is a dual meet at your rival's pool, where hundreds of people may be rooting for your opponent. Here's where concentration skills really pay off. Those fans have no real effect on your ability to perform *other than their ability to break your concentration.*

A third example, and a frequent occurrence in competitive swimming, is the potentially distracting sensation that develops as lactic acid builds up in muscles as they work. This discomfort can be easily tolerated if you have developed the ability to concentrate on those aspects of performance that will determine success. The mind must focus on what it must do to succeed, not on those distractions that can be counterproductive.

One final thought on concentration. One of the ways to determine whether you are in a state of concentration is to ask yourself the question, "Where are my thoughts? Am I in the 'here and now?' " That phrase "here and now" refers to two things: 1. Am I focused on where I am right now, am I *here?* Or is my mind wandering to a different location. 2. Is my mind on *now?* Or am I thinking

about a past or future event or circumstance? The here and now is the only
place where you can affect the outcome of anything. You need to have your
mind *here* and *now.* Those two simple words can tell you a great deal about
the level of your concentration.

To review, then: after you have relaxed your muscles and gotten your
breathing under control, and you've used the key words "Let go" and "Breathe
easy" in conjunction with those processes, you need to find an appropriate
object to concentrate on to bring your mind to a point of focus. I suggest using
the object and word "water." When you have achieved a state of concentration,
begin the final step in the mental preparation process—*visualization.*

VISUALIZATION

While concentration is a difficult concept to grasp, the concept of visualization
should be simple. A visualization is a mental picture—in our case, of what we
want to happen and how it will happen. We all visualize all the time. It is
impossible not to do so. When we are young, we call our visualizations day-
dreams. If you think about it for a moment, we always have pictures of what
we expect to have happen in our lives. Some visualizations are set in the distant
future; others are more current. If we are interested in peak performance, we
must create and control our visualizations of our competitive events and even
our workouts. Visualization is an incredibly powerful tool for achievement in
all phases of our lives.

How does a visualization work? Do you remember how we talked at the
beginning of this chapter about the ability to perform without having to do
everything with the conscious mind? The most fluid, skillful movements are a
product of the subconscious. They are not "thought of," they are simply done
automatically. The part of the subconscious mind that controls this action is
a stored memory called a visualization.

The key to the visualization is that the subconscious mind stores vividly
imagined experiences in the same way that it stores "real" experiences. These
visualizations are there, ready for activation by certain cues which you supply.

It's important to realize that the mind cannot help the body achieve things
for which it *is not physically prepared.* A great visualization will not help a
swimmer with a 500 freestyle best of 5:10 achieve a 4:30. The body is simply
not ready yet. What it will do, however, is allow you to swim as fast and as
well as you are physically prepared to go at a given time.

How do we visualize? A good visualization is very much like a movie.

Think about what makes a good movie. Most people would include the following list of elements:

1. a good plot
2. dialogue
3. color
4. action
5. real, believable characters (and action)
6. a stirring or satisfying conclusion
7. an emotional content

The last item is very important. Emotion is the "glue" that holds the visualization cemented in your subconscious. Now build your visualization for the event you want to think about. What will you do that day? When will you get up? What will your actions be early in the day? Think about whom you will meet, what you will say and do. How do you want to behave? What will happen as the time nears for the meet? How will you get to the site? What will you think and do and say on the way? How will you enter the building, and what mental approach will you take at that point? How will you warm up? Will there be a team meeting? How will you participate? What will be all the little and big things that you will do in the period before your event? Plan, control, and visualize these things. Don't forget to build several different scenarios that you are comfortable with, so you aren't thrown off if the team bus is an hour late and you miss all but 15 minutes of warmup. Prepare for all eventualities. You can overcome any adversity if you have a plan.

Visualizing the Race

Visualizing the race itself is a critical process. You must see yourself doing what you plan to do. There is a famous and accurate saying that goes, "Winners see what they want to happen, and losers see what they fear happening." Plan and see the race in detail. "Feel," mentally, what each stroke and movement will be like. Leave nothing out. Any part you neglect will result in a "blank spot" on the tape, and you will flounder when you reach that point in the race. Again, visualize a variety of scenarios, and how each can turn out positively for you and your goals. There is no one perfect way to achieve your racing goals. There is only a flexible plan that leaves you prepared to cope with any eventuality that brings you the result you seek. Visualize the race with emotion. Feel what you want to feel at each stage of the race. Immerse yourself as much as possible in the feel of the race. Leave nothing to chance. Prepare for everything possible.

What about key or trigger words? As in the rest of the mental preparation process for peak performance, they are important. Try to find a word or phrase that tells you precisely what action you must take at the key juncture to have a successful race. You might want to say, for example, "Fast back half" if you want to negative split the 500 free, that is, swim the second half of the race faster. Or you might say "Push through" on the finish of the stroke if you're a 200 fly sprinter. Or you might say "Third 50" as a key for when to move if you're a 200-meter (or yard) freestyler. Whatever the key to success is in your particular race becomes the key word you should practice in your mental preparation process.

In mental practice, do your visualization in a variety of ways. First, go over it in slow motion and be sure you have included everything you want. Gradually speed it up to normal speed, or even a touch faster. Next, do part of it with your eyes open, and concentrate on doing it right, even with visual distractions. Next, perhaps try it with music or distracting noises around you. Once you think you have your visualization down fairly well, try to go over it a few times during practice. Review the visualization in your mind as you swim. Don't be surprised to find yourself swimming faster and getting excited during these reviews. These are perhaps some of the best times to practice visualizations, as you are both physically and mentally involved, and have distractions around you to practice ignoring.

Remember, *visualize what you want to have happen.* Visualize it vividly, with color and emotion. Know it in precise detail. Leave nothing out. Use your key words frequently, and practice the visualization in a variety of situations and settings.

Now let's review the entire process of mental preparation for peak performance and consider some methods for putting the whole process to effective work for you.

PUTTING IT ALL TOGETHER

Once you have begun developing your relaxation, concentration, and visualization skills, the next step in preparing yourself mentally for peak performance is developing your ability to put the three skills together effectively. The key to putting it all together is utilizing your key words or phrases as "triggers" to bring out the qualities you want to develop. As mentioned earlier, you should try to develop both a long and a short form of mental preparation.

Long-Term Mental Preparation

In swimming, it's useful to look to the end of the season, or to a meet at least several months away, as a target for your mental preparation. When you do that, you should select an event, or events, that you are going to prepare for, and focus your mental preparation on that race. You can begin early in the season, setting appropriate goals and deciding when and where you will "go for it." At first you should begin your mental preparation process in a quiet, nondistracting environment. Many athletes in different sports have found it particularly useful to develop their skills just before going to sleep, and this may possibly aid in both skill retention and visualization.

You can begin your mental preparation process in the same way. When you retire for the night, lie in your bed and go through the muscular relaxation and breath control sequences, remembering to utilize the key commands "Let go" and "Breathe easy." Then move into a concentration exercise, using water or another complex substance or article, and finally, begin visualizing the kind of performance you want to have in the aimed-for meet. It will be helpful if you build "layers" onto the visualization. Begin with a framework of the plot you want, then add details to it, and work hard to "feel" what the experience of winning or racing fast without distraction will be like.

Go through your visualization completely once a day, and utilize your key words or phrase all the time. Once you have mastered the relaxation, breathing, and concentration skills adequately, most of your time will be spent developing and enriching your visualization. Your aim is to leave nothing out that may occur, and to explore mentally how you will react to each situation. By covering every contingency, you are making sure that there will be no psychic surprises in the race. You prepare all of your potential tactics, and prepare for those of your competition as well.

Steady preparation over a lengthy period of time will help you develop what you need to fully prepare for the competition. Mental training is much like physical preparation in this regard. One other point: It is indeed possible to do too much mental rehearsal during the season. This is true because as you will recall, the "glue" that holds the process together is emotion, your emotional input into the visualization. If you practice the race too many times in the days immediately preceding the event, you run the risk of coming in "flat" and emotionally tired. As in many other things athletic, moderation is the key. Stick with your once-a-day visualization procedure right through the meet, and if you find yourself becoming overly "edgy" prior to the event, leave out the visualization and work only on relaxation, breath control, and concentration.

Short-term mental preparation is just as important for a peak performance as the longer-term variety. In competition, or just prior to competition, you should be able to react correctly to unexpected challenges and distractions. No matter how well you prepare mentally, you can be sure, if you are facing quality competition, that others are doing the same quality of mental work as you are. The difference, then, becomes who can focus their efforts on the day of the race while avoiding the inevitable distractions to performance.

Let's look at some specific examples. Let's say you are preparing to race, and you step up onto the blocks and adjust your goggles. As you do so the strap breaks, and you are suddenly 5 seconds from the start of the biggest race of the season, and without your trusty goggles. What do you do? Do you panic and forget your entire plan and lose all that good preparation, or do you do the right thing and calmly raise your hand and ask the referee for an additional moment? Whether you are granted the opportunity to get a second pair of goggles or not, your concentration may be destroyed unless you are skilled in the use of short-term mental preparation.

If you are properly skilled (and drilled), you simply utilize the moment to review and say to yourself your key words: "Let go . . . Breathe easy . . . Water . . . Power," or whatever your key words are. If properly practiced well before the meet, this instant review will cause your body to react as it has been trained to do: your muscles will relax (muscular relaxation), you'll breathe from the belly (belly breathing), you'll refocus on the task at hand (be in the here and now), and your body will be prepared to deliver power to the stroke. It's a simple strategy, isn't it—associating a word with the state that you wish to achieve. But it works. And the most important function of the key words is to bring you back to focus on the event, the here and now, the race itself. Too, during the race, if it is lengthy enough to allow for some thought and evaluation, continue this key-wording process—anything that will keep you focused on your peak performance.

What else can distract or upset you on the day of the race? Lots of things. Here are just a few:

1. The water is too cold (or too warm).
2. The team car or bus is held up in traffic and you are late to warmup.
3. You discover that you have left your warmup suit on over your competition suit.
4. Your girlfriend [boyfriend] is talking with your rival before the race.

5. You note that the sun is in your eyes on backstroke during warmup.

6. There are two false starts in your race before you get to go.

7. The touchpad in your lane has malfunctioned for the four races just before yours.

The list can go on and on. The opportunities for distraction are endless, and you must recognize and develop the power of the short-form mental preparation to combat them. In the final section of this chapter, let's look at some of the types of psych-outs and psych-ups you might face as you mentally prepare for a race.

PSYCH-UPS AND PSYCH-OUTS

Hang around any sports environment for any period of time and you will hear the terms "psych-up" and "psych-out" with numbing regularity. As swimmers, we talk all the time about being psyched up, or after a disappointing performance, about being psyched out. What do these two catch phrases really mean?

Psyching up has to do with mental and physical arousal—how ready you are to compete. An aroused swimmer has an elevated muscle temperature and tone, a raised pulse rate, and attentional control. When you have prepared well mentally, you know that you are psyched up to compete. You can also assist in the psych-up with a number of other mechanisms. One used frequently by athletes of all persuasions is listening to certain types of music. For those who need to increase arousal, upbeat, rock-type, faster-tempo music may be just the thing. For those whose anxiety levels begin to climb as race time approaches, slow, relaxed music may be the key.

A different type of psych-up is to dwell on what you perceive to be the rewards of achieving your goals in the upcoming race. Some swimmers go so far as to discuss these rewards with their friends and teammates before the race.

Team cheers and appreciative words are also psych-ups. There is nothing quite so motivating as the knowledge that your performance will affect the entire team in their performances. Team effort is almost always a key motivator in psyching up the individual. No one likes to let his or her teammates down, and we all like to be thought of as someone who "comes through" under pressure. There are numerous well-known examples in sports history that illustrate the importance of the team in psyching up the individual athlete. Here, the principle to remember is that if you wish your teammates to cheer for you, you must also cheer for your teammates. This collective energy is sometimes referred to as "synergy" and is a tremendously powerful force. We all want to come through for our team, in sports and in life.

You must, however, understand that it's possible to become too "psyched up." Each of us has his or her own individual level of arousal that is proper for peak performance. When we go beyond this point, performance suffers because we overinvolve muscles that we need to perform fine movements, and this in turn disturbs our ability both to concentrate and to coordinate muscularly. Some athletes need remarkably lower levels of arousal than others in order to reach peak performance. We should all be aware of this difference and psych ourselves and others up accordingly. The goal, remember, is to have each swimmer perform at peak and to be optimally, not maximally, stimulated. Know what psychs you up to the proper level, and then plan to do what you must to achieve your psyched-up state prior to your competition. Psyching up should be a positive, rewarding experience.

The other phrase constantly bandied about by athletes of all sorts is the "psych-out." What is a psych-out? In common usage, it is a destructive tactic used by one athlete against another that ruins the concentration and attention of the victim, resulting in seriously damaged performance levels.

How does a psych-out occur? In a number of ways. One of the most interesting types of psych-outs is the one that removes us from our "automatic" mode of operation and forces us to think about our movements. As we have discussed, the most effective actions are those that are programmed into our subconscious and that we do not have to think about. If we do bring these acts to the surface and think about them, we lose the benefit of their automatic action. How does this happen in swimming? Let's say a competitor comes up to you before the race and says, "Fred, congratulations on your butterfly, it's really improved a lot. Are you kicking closer to when you breathe now?" Sounds like a nice compliment right? In reality, a comment like that can cause you to start thinking about when you are kicking, and thereby ruin your newfound improvement just before the race.

Another tactic is to distract the swimmer and disturb his concentration. This can be fairly crude—a deliberate false start, say, or excessive splashing water before a race—or it can be pretty subtle, as in: "Fred, that was a really great 400 IM. Congratulations, you really swam hard. You and I are both in the 200 free in a few minutes, right?" Again, in the guise of a compliment, the word "hard" will stand out in Fred's mind a few minutes after he begins to think how nice it was to receive that compliment. Pretty soon Fred is saying to himself, "Gee, yes, I did swim that kind of hard—actually, really hard—and boy, I am a little tired! How long till the 200?"

The easiest way to avoid a psych-out? Refocus and revisualize the peak performance you wish to attain—in other words, remember your mental training!

A psych-out can be deliberate or it can be accidental. Like many things, its effect is determined by the reaction of the person to whom it is directed. Anything that destroys the ability to concentrate becomes a psych-out if the swimmer allows it to be, and conversely, nothing can psych out the swimmer who is tightly focused on his own race and his own efforts.

There is one key that must be remembered if you suspect that you are the target of another athlete's psych-out attempt. If another swimmer is trying to psych you out, it can only mean one thing: He is not concentrating on his own performance, but on yours. This is actually bad news for him and good news for you! Also, realize that a psych-out attempt is the supreme compliment, since the other swimmer obviously feels that the only way he can outperform you is to throw you off your best effort. That should help provide you with considerable confidence in your own abilities.

Whether deliberate or accidental, psych-outs can happen. When they do, you need to retain the presence of mind to properly combat them with the peak performance skills that you have learned. Simply *recenter* and *refocus* with your short form of the peak performance techniques. This mental "shakeout" will allow you to perform at your best and confidently execute what you have so painstakingly visualized.

The occasional deliberate psych-out effort by another athlete reveals a shallow grasp of the real benefits and philosophical strengths of our sport. In the final chapter, we will explore the idea of competition and relate it to your growth as an athlete and as a person. By the end of that discussion, I hope you will recognize that the idea of a deliberate psych-out truly has no place in our sport of swimming. All of our efforts should be directed to individual peak performance through optimum mental and physical preparation.

8

Competition and Beyond

WHAT IS COMPETITION?

No matter how proficient you become at the various swimming strokes, or how good your swimming conditioning, some of the finer satisfactions of swimming will be hidden from you until you experience competition. Whether you are 8 years old or 80, you will find the deepest satisfactions in the personal challenges of swimming in competition.

The derivation of the word "competition" reveals the most satisfying part of the experience. From ancient Greek, the word comes from two roots meaning "to strive with." Both words are important. *To strive* is to try mightily, and *with* indicates a cooperative effort alongside your fellow competitor. The swimming experience mirrors this definition perfectly.

Starting simultaneously from a dive off the starting platform and swimming in parallel lanes, competitors stimulate each other to ever more substantial efforts in speed and endurance. When we compete, we truly "strive with" our opponent. This "striving with" has many significant implications that we will explore in this chapter.

What about the very young child? There are an abundance of horror stories about "Little League syndrome": overinvolved parents and coaches whose personal egos and interests interfere with their children's enjoyment of any sport. Swimming has had its share of these problems also. But far more numerous are the hundreds of thousands of age-group swimming families who have had lasting social and educational experiences of the highest caliber through swimming. As in most other sports activities, the proper attitude by both parent and swimmer goes a long way toward a healthy enjoyment of competition. Later in this chapter, we will spend some time discussing some of

True competition means "striving with" our opponents.

the philosophies of competitive swimming that I feel have withstood the test of time, certainly here in America.

During a swimmer's early years (age 10 through college), there are numerous opportunities for competition at all levels. These include park, district, and country club teams, junior and senior high school teams, YMCA and United States Swimming Club teams, and finally, collegiate swimming at all calibers from the most serious and challenging to the most casual.

The older swimmer has the opportunity for the longest career of all. Organized masters swimming now exists for those swimmers from the age of 21 up. Every fifth birthday is extra cause for celebration as you become the "youngster upstart" in the next age group. The opportunities for meaningful competition and travel at the masters level are now huge, with masters swimming growing at an astonishing rate worldwide. For the master swimmer, the health and fitness benefits transcend those of any other activity; only cross-country skiing is on the same par. Competition keeps interest in masters swimming high, and the stimulation to "be the very best you can be" at a meet sometimes seems to reach a fever pitch. The quality of performances turned in by masters swimmers is truly amazing; many 40-year-olds and older turn in better times than they did as collegians a generation earlier. Competition can indeed turn the clock back for many mature swimmers!

WHERE SHOULD I COMPETE?

There are many different types of competitive swimming experiences available to people in the United States. We are one of the few countries in the world where radically different types of organizations conduct swimming competitions. In most countries, one central swimming organization conducts the competitions available to young people. Our organizational diversity is a real strength for American swimming, reflecting as it does our freedom and individuality, even though it has its drawbacks relative to national swim planning and consistency.

When looking for a program, the first thing you as a swimmer or a swimming family must do is analyze your needs. If you are young and untutored in swimming skills, a program that emphasizes teaching is the right choice. When you have acquired some experience and instruction, it is sometimes best to find a program that offers more challenge in the way of physical training. Finally, as you mature in swimming, it becomes very important to train with a peer group that shares your goals and needs. Finding the right "match" can be tricky, and you and your parents should make a thorough and careful examination of a variety of programs before choosing one with which to affiliate.

What types of programs are available? Many. Below you will find a few of them, with some common characteristics of each type. Naturally, individual programs will reflect different coaching styles, philosophies, and emphasis. What follows is intended strictly as a generalized guideline.

Country Club Programs
Summer Recreation Programs

Most competitive swimmers in this country get started in some form of summer swimming program, frequently right out of learn-to-swim lesson programs. Competitive swimming coaches are always watching the lesson programs for youngsters who demonstrate good natural talent. These programs can vary tremendously in every aspect, including organization, level of coaching talent and experience, degree of seriousness, and award and reward structure. One thing to examine carefully is how enjoyable and satisfying the program seems to be. Are the young swimmers just racing, or are they being taught good skills and ideals? At the younger ages, remember, you should seek a program that provides good instruction and education as well as an enjoyable experience. Look for a program that stresses *learning* as well as *winning*. Most of the summer programs feature a dual meet-type of format, with just two teams competing, and later in the summer a league-type of championship. Even the fees for these programs can vary tremendously, from near nothing for public recreation programs to hundreds and even thousands of dollars for some country club teams. Usually these programs are strictly summer experiences, and a two-month swim season is a good indicator of interest at a young age.

YMCA Programs

The National YMCA conducts swimming programs at all levels from learn-to-swim through national competition, and the annual YMCA National Meet is one of the most exciting team-oriented meets in the country. These teams practice and compete either year-round or during the winter months only. The YMCA has a long history of successful and enjoyable competitive swimming programs. They generally revolve around the dual meet concept between Y's, with an age-group program of events.

The YMCA program also includes competitions at the end of the indoor season that include a district and state series leading to a national meet for senior swimmers. In most areas, Y swimmers who are age-groupers can compete right through the state level. In the past several years, the YMCA has offered a summer championship season as well as a traditional meet, and the role of the Y swim program is rapidly expanding.

YMCA swimming is usually very affordable for a family. The level of coaching in the YMCAs is a step up from most summer swimming, and many of our nation's greatest coaches have gotten their start in the Y program. Unfortunately, because the YMCA salary scale is relatively low, the talented Y coaches frequently (though not always) move on to another level of swimming where the financial reward is more satisfying. Overall, the YMCA program is an excellent choice for the young swimmer.

High School Swimming

For athletes of the appropriate age, high school swimming can be a tremendous experience. The team involvement and four-year tradition that often evolve can be both socially and psychologically rewarding, as well as an opportunity for fast and exciting swimming. The quality of high school swimming varies tremendously across the nation, from mediocre to superb. Sport history in the region, support from YMCA and club feeder programs, and the availability of quality coaches all contribute to the variety that exists. High school swimming usually involves dual meet formats, with a series that encompasses district and state competitions for teams and/or individuals. In strong swimming states such as Indiana, Florida, and California, the high school state meet is *the* swimming event of the year. In schools where the team is tied to a strong year-round program, a marvelous opportunity exists for young people to expand their potential to the maximum. Coordination of school and community programs is a real priority item to be addressed across the nation.

One major drawback to high school swimming is that it can attract too much attention to an athlete too early, and true talent can stop short of real development when a high school state championship is achieved early in a career. In some areas, such achievement can come relatively easily, and unless other swimming avenues are explored, the swimmer may be satisfied with an achievement far short of that of which he or she is capable. High school swimmers who experience success need reminders that there are 50 states out there, and *each* has a state champion. When the magnitude of an accomplishment can be kept in perspective, high school swimming has a tremendous amount to offer the young athlete.

Collegiate Swimming

College swimming comes in at least three varieties. Division I is the "upper" division, with very fast swimmers on scholarship for their athletic talent (though many Division I swimmers are *not* on scholarship, and most Division I coaches welcome non-scholarship swimmers who are willing to conform to tough team standards). The national meets are the showcase of the sport in the wintertime, and have very difficult standards. To make it to the Division I national meet, a swimmer must be almost a world-class athlete. Those who do not make the nationals usually end their season at the conference meet following a dual meet schedule. One positive aspect of Division I swimming is the usually superb sports-medicine and scientific support that is available to the swimmer.

There are two other collegiate divisions, II and III. Division II has some scholarships, some support, and limited resources to devote to the sport. Division III is strictly non-scholarship, with athletes participating solely for their personal enjoyment. The coaching available in each division ranges the full spectrum from adequate to excellent. One can find outstanding coaches in Division III and merely adequate ones in Division I. Generally speaking, the larger schools tend to be Division I or II, and the smaller schools Division III, but there are exceptions. Once again, the range of diversity is impressive, and any prep or high school swimmer willing to do his homework on college options will find a blend of academics and swimming that will be highly rewarding and satisfying. Junior-college swimming and NAIA (National Association of Intercollegiate Athletics) schools are two other potential avenues for the post–high school swimmer.

United States Swimming

The national governing body of our sport, so denominated by Congress, United States Swimming (USS) organizes the international teams of the United States and prepares teams for the Olympics and World Championships, in addition to conducting the largest participation programs in the swimming world in terms of numbers. With both age-group and senior athletes involved, USS counts over 200,000 members. Competition ranges from the very novice to the Olympic team. The teams themselves are usually referred to as "club" teams, though they are almost always open to the general public. Because they offer greater financial reward, clubs usually attract many of the best coaches for athletes of all ages. Club swimming does range from highly competitive to very relaxed, but offers the possibility of a youngster progressing all the way to the very top of swimming's ladder, the Olympic Games and World Championships. USS is truly "open" swimming, with no other membership beyond USS necessary to participate. Fees for team membership vary widely and generally reflect the level of opportunity open to the athlete in the club. USS swimming philosophically is dedicated to allowing the athlete to go as far as he or she desires. USS clubs stress a variety of different concerns, and careful investigation will let you determine which club is most suited to your needs. United States Swimming is dedicated to becoming both the biggest (encompassing large numbers in the benefits of the sport) and the best (international supremacy) in the world.

Masters Swimming

Both the YMCA and United States Masters Swimming, Inc., operate programs for adults that are divided into age groups and offer frequent competitions. Many USS clubs across the country offer programs that are affiliated with one or both of the national programs. In masters swimming, the benefits and values focus on health and fitness and not on competitive victory. Masters swimming is the fastest-growing section of the sport today. If you are an adult swimmer, masters is for you!

The names, addresses, phone numbers, and contact persons for all the organizations described above are listed in the back of this book.

WITH WHOM SHOULD I COMPETE?

Whom to compete with is one of those questions that sounds so easy, yet has such complicated answers with profound implications. It is a question that both parents and young swimmers need to spend considerable time thinking about. The answer goes back to why you decided to become a swimmer in the first place.

If you are a swimmer because it keeps you healthy and involved with a good set of friends, fine; it's certainly one of the major reasons that people take up swimming, and many are happy keeping their involvement at that level. If that's your reason for swimming, you should be seeking a level of competition that makes you happy, among equally uncompetitive, like-minded swimmers. You will not be happy in a highly competitive group.

Many young people who start in the sport for social reasons develop a

different attitude in which they eventually wish to become the very best swimmer that they can be. In doing so, they become very competitive and eager for
challenges and tests. Alternatively, and sadly, this can sometimes become
twisted into a desire simply to be successful. There is a world of difference
between these two attitudes.

There are countless Olympic swimmers who have rarely won a race. And
there are many more swimmers who have won most of the races they have
entered, and never progressed even to a state championship level of performance. How often you win is not your measure as a swimmer, but rather the times
of your performances and whom you are competing against. One of the most
disheartening things in swimming is the athlete who "could have been," had
he had the guidance to seek quality competition.

If you decide to dedicate yourself to becoming the best swimmer that you
can be, whom should you compete with? First of all, you must realistically look
for people who are slightly better than you are. Putting a novice swimmer in
with a state champion is not necessarily good for either one. You must be able
to experience some success in training and in races with your competitors.
Remember the meaning of the word competition: to "strive with." You must
find people who will stimulate your performance to higher levels. You do
indeed become like those with whom you associate. If you want to be a great
swimmer, you must first be a good swimmer, so train and compete with those
slightly better than you are. Remember that competition needs to begin in
workout, where the improvement occurs, as well as in the meet, where the
capabilities are measured.

As soon as you experience success in a group, or at one level of competition, you need to move up a notch to the next level. If you are totally dominating one type of meet or level of swimming, you have already wasted valuable
time that you could have been using to "grow" against stiffer competition.
Everyone needs his chance to shine, to win a race, to be recognized. Be sure
that you don't become so enamored of competitive success that you neglect to
strive further.

Anyone can build up a great winning record by competing against mediocre opponents. Remember that you are trying to become the very best that you
can be. You can do that only by challenging yourself with better competition.
At first each new level with be difficult and challenging, but you will adapt
physically and psychologically, and soon be comfortable at that level, and
eventually you will begin to achieve success at the new level. *Compete with those
athletes more accomplished than you, and aspire to be the best! Everyone is
capable of being his or her own best self!*

THE ROLE OF THE COACH

One of the best people to help you in your development as a swimmer is your coach. Coaches come in many different styles, abilities, and interests, just like anything else in the world. You'll want to choose a good coach for yourself, to help you gain the things you want from competitive swimming. For younger athletes, there are three important people in the pyramid of success: the coach, the parents, and the athletes themselves. For older athletes, success can simply become an equation involving just the coach and the athlete. What do you want a coach for?

First of all, for instruction. The coach is a professional who has a deep knowledge of swimming and its techniques, training, and competition. The coach also has a wellspring of experience that you can draw on to avoid making the same mistakes that others have made before you. In practice, it is important to understand how to "use" your coach to best advantage. The coach is your eyes and ears on the deck; he can see things and relay instructions to you based on what he sees, which you might not notice in the water. He can offer ideas on stroke improvement and drills to help you practice properly. Remember: You want to learn from the coach, not to impress him with how much you know. Coaches see thousands of swimmers each year. They're acutely aware of just how skilled or unskilled you may be. Concentrate on listening and absorbing what your coach has to offer.

Second, most coaches are skilled trainers. They will design and direct workouts that will develop you physically. When you have a coach who is a good trainer, he will build a progressive program that will be physically challenging, even exhausting, but that will strengthen you over the season and bring you to a peak performance at some stage. Coaches will usually not only give you the "set" or work to be done, but will tell you how it is to be accomplished. Pay particular attention to the directions for each set, and do your best to follow them to the letter. If you plunge ahead, ignoring directions, you'll be a lot like someone trying to put a jigsaw puzzle together without a picture to guide him. The coach has a particular plan, and how each workout is swum is a part of it. If the coach does not share that plan with you, it can be a good idea to ask him to do so. That will sometimes give you a clearer picture of where you are going during the season.

Third, a coach can be a source of inspiration. A coach with experience, either personal competitive experience or in coaching, can provide you with a number of interesting and stimulating experiences or help you gain perspective on the achievability of your goals. Most coaches are genuinely interested in the

A good coach is an instructor, a trainer, a resource in preparing swimmers for competition, and a source of inspiration.

individuals they coach. Coaching is not a rewarding profession financially, and many talented people coach purely because they enjoy working with people and helping them achieve their personal goals. A coach can be a good and long-term friend.

Finally, a coach is an invaluable resource in preparing you for competition. Right now, we are going to explore how coaches function at swim meets with their teams. We will describe what you should expect from your coach, what you could expect, and what you might receive from your coach. And we will ask you to play an important part in the process of a swim meet also.

The Coach at Swim Meets

When your coach accompanies you to swim meets, you have a fabulous opportunity to improve, which you should capitalize upon. The most significant thing your coach can provide you with is an objective evaluation of your performance.

Most coaches will discuss with the athlete before the race what the goals and objectives of that particular swim should be. These might include a personal-best time, a particular race strategy, a technique to be worked on, or any of a number of other race objectives. This opportunity to review with your coach what you are trying to accomplish provides an excellent cue to help you bring your task into focus. Indeed, you might wonder why you would ever start a race without a clear objective firmly in mind. The results of this discussion, then, become how you will later evaluate your swim. As you compete, the coach will be watching your swim so that later he can offer suggestions and ideas on how successfully you achieved your aims, and how you might improve the next time. What the coach is able to bring you that nobody else can is *accurate technical feedback.*

That, in a nutshell, should be the role of your coach at a swim meet. If you receive good technical feedback relating to yor goals, the coach has been a great help. No other person can offer you this feedback, and it should be highly valued.

Mom, Dad, siblings, boy- or girlfriends can cheer and offer encouragement to you, and others can bring you the kind of recognition that you enjoy, but *only your coach* can provide you with useful technical feedback. And only information can tell you how to do better the next time.

Now let's look at this swim meet picture from the coach's point of view. Let's say that your team has 20 swimmers at the meet. What does the coach have to do at a minimum? If the coach deals the same way with each swimmer, he has to offer advice and counsel before each race, then observe each swimmer closely, taking split times and making notes on each person, then discuss and evaluate the race afterwards with each athlete. Can you understand why this can sometimes be a confusing, challenging, and frustrating job for your coach? All coaches do their very best to help each of their swimmers at a meet, but with that enormous number of tasks, it's easy to make mistakes, miss people, or simply not see everything. Swim meets are very concentration-intensive times for swim coaches.

Why should you care about that? Because sometimes it is easy to forget all that the coach has to do, and to focus too intensely on your own races and the coach's response to them. You feel intensely about your efforts. The coach has to do a great job with 20 people, while you are responsible for one. Remember that, and try not to monopolize the coach's time and attention nor to expect emotional reactions to your successes. The coach's primary role is an objective evaluator, and if he has time and energy to offer cheerleader encouragement or personal attention, that's a bonus. It's also an unreasonable expectation. The encouragement and cheers should come from your teammates. If you have the type of team where that is not done, and you want it to happen, remember that those who cheer for others *get* cheered themselves.

You at Swim Meets

Earlier we said we would ask you to play a part in the process of competing in the meet as well as swimming your events. This part is vital to your long-term swimming success. Later in this chapter we will elaborate further on this role, but it's so important that it bears saying twice.

Simply put, when you are at a swim meet, one of the most successful things you can do is to act as your own swim coach. As we mentioned, with a number of athletes competing in a meet in rapid sequence, there is no way that you will receive the amount of attention from a coach that we all would like. That means that *you have to learn to help yourself to a great degree.* The aim of most swim coaches is to work themselves out of a job, to make their swimmers so independent as they get older that the coach is needed less and less.

In acting as your own coach, probably the most important thing that you will do is to view the swim meet as a time to analyze and evaluate what you intend to do, and then to review your actual performance. That requires taking an intellectual and objective point of view of your performance, rather than an emotional and subjective one. Sometimes that's very difficult, but it relates to how you view your whole swimming career and your life. In an upcoming section, "Some Philosophy for Competitive Swimming," we will discuss a number of ideas that I feel you should incorporate into your swimming thinking to help you achieve the intellectual, objective viewpoint that is necessary for long-term success. Once you can incorporate these ideas into your swimming approach, you will be on your way to a rapidly increasing rate of satisfaction with your performances. Even more, you will come to deeply appreciate the role of your swim coach, both during competition and throughout your entire career.

RACE STRATEGIES

For every swim meet, you will want to develop a plan or strategy of how to swim your races. As you mature in the sport, you will recognize that your strategies will change with your maturity, the moment in the season, your physical condition, the competition, the significance of the race itself, and many other factors. Essentially, race strategies become very individual over time, with each person choosing what he thinks works well for him in each set of circumstances. One quality that you will want to cultivate in yourself is the knack for utilizing a variety of strategies effectively.

In swimming history, there are numerous great swimmers who never won "The Big One." In many instances, this is because they could swim with only one type of strategy, and their opponents recognized that any strategy can be countered effectively if the competitors are of relatively equal ability (and lesser swimmers can defeat superior ones if they take advantage of better tactics in certain situations). Your goal, then, as a racer, is to become comfortable with a range of tactics so that you can be effective in a variety of conditions.

In important races, swimmers will usually focus on one of two main goals. The first goal might be to finish first or among the top three. (In some cases a swimmer will swim tactically to place third, or whatever, to advance to a final. This lets the swimmer complete the preliminaries with a minimum of effort.) We will refer to that as *swimming for place*. The second possibility is to swim for a personal-best time. This we will call *swimming for time*.

These two possibilities and their various combinations cover the major objectives of most important swims. It's important to note that tactics and strategies for each of the two can sometimes be noncomplementary or even counterproductive. The swimmer who tries to advance to the final and is

In preparing a race strategy, most competitive swimmers choose to swim either for place or for time.

satisfied with an outside lane assignment will surely not put in a major effort, and in this tactical kind of race the swimmer will not record a personal best. Similarly, the swimmer who elects to go for a best time will likely select a race strategy that may make him vulnerable to another swimmer who chooses to swim strictly to win the race.

There are times and places for both types of objectives and for all types of strategies. When involved in hotly contested dual meets, the swimmer might be letting the team down if he committed to a tactic that would help him swim fast but not win the race. There are times when winning is the paramount goal. Olympic swimmers in the Olympic final will usually be most concerned with having the gold medal put around their necks in the evening final, yet may elect a best-time type of strategy in the morning preliminaries in order to ensure themselves a place in the final. Most developing swimmers in ordinary meets will choose strategies that optimize their chances for best times, since times are truly the best indicator of personal progress in the sport.

We will now proceed to explain, in classic, simple terms, the various strategies and tactics that swimmers may employ. In real swimming experiences, these ideas frequently blend to best suit the individual athlete. Remember, your primary goal as a developing swimmer is to become comfortable with any and all of these possibilities.

Strategies for a Fast Time

There are three accepted strategies for a swimmer who is going after a best time. Each is dependent on individual strengths to be successful, and each must be systematically practiced if it is to be of use to the swimmer in the quest for a personal best.

The Physiology Solution. Any exercise physiologist will tell you one solution for a best time strategy: the evenly paced race. Science has shown that, in all but the very shortest distances, the evenly paced race, with all intermediate times the same (with the compensation for the dive on the first length), will result in the best application of physical energy and the fastest times. In theory at least, these "even-split" races are races to "beat the clock." Experimentation will tell you if this is a good strategy for you.

A Psychological Solution. Many swimmers, especially in the shorter races, prefer to go out fast early in the race. They do this for a variety of valid reasons, including the opportunity to swim in calm water, to get away from the distracting presence of their opponents, and especially to get themselves in an excellent position at the halfway point in the swim. Being considerably "to the good" side (that is, ahead of pace) of an even-paced split in a short race can be a real psychological upper and can enhance the swimmer's ability to motivate himself through the pain barriers late in the race. In many short races, those swimmers who are going for a best time try to "take it out fast."

A Psychological Alternative. In the longer races, and even in many of the 200-yard or -meter races, some swimmers prefer the tactic of a negative split or negative effort race strategy in order to achieve a best time. *Negative split* means that the actual time of the second half of the race is faster than the first half, and negative effort means that regardless of actual time, the swimmer exerts considerably more effort in the second half. Frequently, both ideas result in the same effect on the "splits" of the race, though they may be described independently. There are some of the same sound principles of physiology involved here as in the even-split tactic, but it can be very psychologically stimulating to be coming from behind in relatively "fresh" shape when the opponent is beginning to tire. For the aggressive and confident swimmer, this is often a highly successful tactic.

All of these tactics have been time-tested and found to be suitable for a best-time swim. All three have to be rehearsed and physically prepared for in very specific workouts and with realistic simulation in practice. As in most other things in swimming, superior preparation will prevail.

Strategies for a Victory

When a swimmer is involved in a race where his or her finishing place in it is of greater consideration than the time, some different tactical considerations need to be made. The three strategies listed for a best time can also be used effectively to race to win. Each has its limitations. The even-split strategy can wear an opponent down and physically take it out of him. It's an appropriate strategy if the swimmer is confident that he is in superior physical condition relative to his opponent. In contrast, it is a dangerous choice when competing with a superior or equally prepared opponent, because it leaves the opponent with the relatively easier task of following closely, then mounting an offensive charge to dominate late in the race. Almost all swimmers or endurance athletes find it easier to follow closely than to lead. The leader of a close race pays a heavier physical and psychological burden. The "fast out" strategy can also be an excellent one when employed with an opponent who is easily discouraged by your early show of speed. It can be disastrous against a tenacious opponent, who will merely keep contact until you begin to tire. Some classic races have resulted when a "fast out" swimmer confronts a swimmer who employs the negative split strategy. The negative split strategy is for the strong, endurance-based swimmer who is confident of his ability to increase the tempo and actual pace of the race sufficiently to catch his opponent at the end. When negative splitting, it is possible to get too far behind too early, or to misjudge the opponent's tactic—he may also be negative splitting. If that is the case, the race can turn into a frantic sprint for the finish.

Some other tactics for middle- and distance-oriented swimmers: *Surge and relax tactics.* This means a series of short accelerations to test the response of the opponent, while retaining physical control of one's own race. When a weakness is sensed in the response, the swimmer makes a longer surge to establish a substantial lead, and then retains that lead and effort to the end. There is an effective pattern that divides a race of any distance into quarters, to combine the physiology and psychology implicit in several of the above concepts. Let's say the swimmer swims very fast for the first 30 seconds of the race (fast-out theory), then backs off the accelerator for the next quarter of the race and regains physiological control. After the halfway point he gradually accelerates to the finish. This is a clever and sophisticated use of physiology, because it first uses the available "first gear" energy system that will be burned anyway to establish a substantial first split (and usually a lead), then backs off into a physiological comfort zone, and gradually accelerates the use of the energy stores, which moves his body into lactate production and lactate tolerance as the race proceeds. From the opponent's point of view, the swimmer using this tactic establishes a dominating position; then, when the opponent fights back into contention, the first swimmer accelerates away again. This is an excellent use of all we know physiologically and psychologically to win a race. Again, it demands practice and preparation.

Whether you swim to win or swim for time, you must develop a plan, prepare for the plan, and finally, execute the plan. Whether best time or first place is your goal, your real opponent is yourself, and your real ally is how well you can imagine, prepare, and execute.

WHAT TO DO AFTER A COMPETITION

In a word, after participating in a competition, you should *analyze.*

One of the most important things that you can learn as a swimmer is that *the way to improve is to intellectually evaluate your performance after each swim, meet, and season.* If you only react with happiness or frustration after each swim, you cannot learn from either your excellent swims or your failures. The key is *learning* from each competitive effort.

After Each Race

You should go into each racing event with a goal. As we have discussed before, the goals can be anything from a best time, to a stroke improvement, to an attitude or approach to the swim. After the event, you need to take a few moments immediately to ask yourself if you achieved your goal. If you did, you can then further analyze what good or not-so-good things you did during the swim, and set an idea of a goal for the next time you swim that event, based on your positive experience. If you did not attain your goal yet, you need to analyze what kept you from doing so and formulate your own opinion why that was the case. Your next action is to plan how to correct whatever it was that kept you from your goal. Remember that the best technical resource that you have is your coach. Your coach should be the first person you communicate with in a significant way after the swim, when it is fresh in both your mind and his.

One of the most important things *not* to do after a race is to react emotionally. No one race will make or break your career; whether you are happy or sad, the emotion will be short-lived. In addition to being poor sportsmanship, emotional reactions interfere with the important process of getting accurate technical feedback on what you should do next time.

Finally, remember that almost everyone you meet will be encouraging to you after you swim. Many people will tell you "Good swim" or words to that effect, whether it really was a good swim or not. Learn to accept compliments gracefully whether in your mind you have earned them or not. The people offering the compliments are well-intentioned and are offering encouragement, recognition, and support for your efforts. Take the time to appreciate their support.

After the Swim Meet

The time after each meet is another excellent period to reflect on your planning and efforts. Your coach may well review the performance with you individually, or with the team as a group, and you will want to do your own review. Here are some things to think about after a meet:

1. How was your rest the week before the meet? The night before the meet?

2. What were your eating habits for the same periods? Did you avoid sugar and concentrate on good carbohydrates?

3. What was your mental approach and buildup to the meet? Was that satisfactory, or do you need a higher or lower activation level?

4. How was your warmup? Did you do all that you needed? Too little? Too much? Enough pace work? Enough kicking?

5. How did you swim each race? Did you let one performance affect the next, or were you able to isolate each experience and then build on the successful ones?

6. How was your communication with your coach and teammates? Did you allow them to function as supports for your efforts, and did you support theirs?

7. Did you *analyze* rather than *emotionalize?*

8. Overall, did you reach your goals for the meet?

9. Finally, have you reset your goals for the next meet and begun your plans to improve?

If you did all of the above, you have had a successful meet even if you didn't swim as fast as you wanted to.

After the Season

At the end of the swim season and prior to the next season, it is important for you to sit down, first by yourself and then with your coach, and review and analyze both the season you have just completed and the one that lies ahead. You need to formulate your own thoughts first, then discuss them with your coach. In some areas the coach may concur; in others he may differ. Remember that the coach has watched a number of swimming careers, and his experience is a valuable resource in helping you understand and appreciate what has transpired during the season.

Again, there are a number of areas you will want to consider:

• *Look at your goals.* Did you achieve all of them, or just a few? Goal setting is designed to be a challenge. If you achieved all of them, maybe you need a greater challenge in the next season. It is equally defeating not to make any of your goals. Seek a balance.

• *Look at what you did in the pool.* How much of each type of work did you actually get down? Did you attend the number of workouts your coach 231 recommended? How honest was your pool effort?

- *What about dry-land training?* Did you do half, three quarters, or nearly all that you were asked to do? Do you think you are stronger or more flexible? How have both been measured? Do you know objectively what you have accomplished? Should you know at the end of next season?

- *How about "hidden training"?* Did you rest properly? Did you allow your body to recover from the effects of hard training and competition? Did you get enough sleep and avoid anything that could hurt your performance?

- *Did you consistently and effectively communicate with your coach(es)?* If not, why not? What can you do about that? Ask the same question with regard to your teammates. How can you be a better team member next season? How can you contribute to the success of the group as well as your own success?

- *What about nutrition?* How consistent were you in adhering to an athletic dietary plan? Are you over- or underweight? How can you adjust?

- *What are your general and specific strengths as a swimmer?* Do you learn well? Can you learn well? What do you need to learn and how will you learn it, and from whom? How do you feel about your mental and emotional approach to the sport? Do you need some mental readjustment? Who can provide that for you?

The point of this postseason evaluation and analysis is not to make yourself feel bad, but rather to encourage yourself about how far you have come, and to educate yourself as to what's next. Swimming is a great sport because an intelligent, analytical athlete can compete favorably with a physically gifted one, if he or she will only apply as much mental as physical effort. The postseason analysis serves as both a review and a preview, and will be the most effective motivator for each person to achieve all he is capable of in the season to come. Use it each and every season, and you will find yourself becoming a skilled analyzer and, over time, your own best coach.

SOME PHILOSOPHY FOR COMPETITIVE SWIMMING

When looking at a swimming career, whether it be your own or that of a friend, a youngster whom you are coaching, or your child, it's helpful to have some guiding principles to reflect upon at moments of indecision. Here are some considerations about competitive swimming that you might find useful.

- *It is possible to practice anything.* You can practice perfection, or you can practice sloppiness. The way you practice will be the way you compete.
- *Courage in competition is a small thing built of many other small things.* Every time you do something correctly, you put a brick in your wall of courage. Every time you do something you shouldn't, you tear a brick out.
- *Competitive victories can be gained against an inferior opponent.* Your toughest opponent will always be your own best effort.
- *A career in swimming is what matters, not one race nor one meet, nor one season. Consistency is what gets the job done.*
- *When you reach one goal, you must immediately reset your goal.* Raise your ambition. The journey to the goal is always more satisfying than the arrival.
- *Competition stimulates you to your best effort.* Seek to compete with the best, in practice and in meets. Use your competitors to motivate yourself, and encourage them to use you. You will become like those with whom you compete.
- *Support your teammates.* Without their help and competition, you could never reach your own best level.
- *Develop slowly, steadily, and persistently in all ways.* Never give up. Breakthroughs are made by those who keep going when others let up.
- *Nobody ever catches up with someone ahead of him by doing less than the leader.*
- *Know the reason behind everything you do.* Have a purpose behind each workout, each race. One of your most important goals should be to work toward becoming a knowledgeable, independent athlete.
- *Enthusiasm is contagious.* If you need some, get close to someone who has some. If someone else needs some, give them some of yours. Nothing great was ever accomplished without enthusiasm.
- *Nobody knows what you want or what you need until you tell them.* Communicate with those whose assistance you need.
- One of the principles of human growth is that we don't know what we want or need until someone tells us what is possible. *Remain open to suggestions or ideas about your sport.*
- *Nobody gets anywhere on his own.* It takes teamwork and help from others. Accept help from and offer help to others. Recognize those who have helped you.
- *Strive to learn what factors make you successful.* Maximize those assets.
- *Strive to learn the factors that restrict your progress,* and work to minimize them.

- *Improvement is the key to everything.* Nothing is impossible; it just takes longer and greater effort.

- *Eliminate the words "I can't" from your vocabulary.* If you must express a frustration, try the phrase "I can't *yet*." Better yet, use "I'll keep trying."

- *Remember that we all act, in the final analysis, according to the picture of ourself that we carry with us, our "self-image."* Change the self-image and you can change the behavior. This is much easier than forcing oneself to go against one's self-image. Build your behavior and performance around the *best* that you have done in any area.

- *All of us are "people who swim," not "swimmers."* We must behave first of all as people in all our relationships. Then as we do a good job of that, it is easy to be a good swimmer.

- *All of us in the United States are free to make choices.* No one has to train. If you choose to train, remember that it is a choice that you have made.

- *If all you do is swimming, what can you bring to swimming?* Train in the pool, then mentally get away from the sport when out of the pool, but don't behave in a manner that contradicts your efforts in the pool! Use other activities and intellectual stimulation to bring new energy and enthusiasm to training.

- *Recognize that there are no shortcuts, no magic.* Talent, perseverance, and consistent hard work will bring results.

- *"Imagine, Prepare, Compete":* the sequence to success.

- *The fastest path to the top is through the most difficult terrain.* The fastest way to excel in swimming is to make the tough event the event you swim the best.

Swimming is a magnificent sport for athletes of all abilities and interests. Whatever *your* goals, think them through, plan your efforts, and be relentless in your pursuit.

Be bold.

PUSHING BACK THE "EDGE"

In any endeavor, it's exciting to speculate on what's next. In swimming this is especially so, because the possibilities are truly remarkable. In the United States, swimming is the most popular of all participation sports, and this popularity holds great potential for explosive growth and development.

Right now, for example, we have four competitive swimming strokes, and we know of at least four other styles of swimming both old and new. When will

Imagine, Prepare, Compete: the sequence to follow for success as a swimmer.

we add another stroke? What will it be? Maybe it will be a corkscrew stroke, or an alternating butterfly-backstroke motion. Perhaps in freestyle, the swimmers of the future will hold their arms out straight from the shoulders and spin like a top through the water (the shoulder development would be spectacular!). Perhaps we will allow the individual medley to be swum in any order that the swimmer chooses. Any number of biomechanical changes are out there, waiting for *you* to discover them and propose them to the rest of the swimming world!

Perhaps in swim meets of the future, we will swim by a combination of height and weight rather than age. All similarly sized athletes will compete together, rather than age groups. Perhaps swimmers will have handicap races based on prior performances. In the nationals, perhaps swimmers will be further restricted on how many events they can swim . . . or perhaps all restrictions will be removed. Can you imagine a swimmer winning (or even competing) in every event at the nationals? Perhaps ways will be found to fund swim clubs other than through swim meets, so meets can be conducted purely for great competition.

Will there be professional swimming? Why not? What will that be like? Marathon swimmers do it now, why not pool swimmers?

What will the science of the future look like? Will we be able to go to a swim center and have our stroke, our physiology, and our psychology adjusted by computers and science tools, just as our automobiles are tuned now? Will we be able to train shorter hours for greater reward? Will we have to train longer to swim faster?

How about the swim coaches of the future? Will they have to be scientists? Physiologists? Psychologists? Biomechanists? Or will they need more managerial skills to use all of the above? Perhaps the swim coaches of the future will have to be better businesspeople so that their teams can afford all the new tools of the trade.

Physiologists tell us that many of our best physical endurance gains can be made when we are 11 to 14 years of age. Will we spend huge amounts of time training at that age in the future, and then less later on?

Will the administrative bodies of swimming ever pull together as one to eliminate all artificial impediments to the optimum progress rate of the elite athlete? Will American swimming continue its world-dominant position, or will American swimming weaken?

I hope that you, as a swimmer, a coach, or a parent of a young swimmer, will be a part of helping to answer these questions. Swimming, to me, is the greatest sport in the world! I hope you'll always be a part of it.

Resources

There are many excellent resources available for those who would like to learn more about competitive swimming. Here are some of the periodicals and organizations that you might want to consult for more information.

Periodicals

Journal of Swimming Research. This magazine provides in-depth articles on the latest in swimming biomechanics and technique. (American Swimming Coaches Association, 1 Hall of Fame Dr., Ft. Lauderdale, FL 33316).

Swim (Swimming World Publications, P.O. Box 45497, Los Angeles, CA 90045). This is an excellent swimming magazine for Masters swimmers and for fitness swimmers of all ages.

Swimming Technique (Swimming World Publications, P.O. Box 45497, Los Angeles, CA 90045). The official publication of the American Swimming Coaches Association, with useful technical information for any swim coach.

Swimming World and Junior Swimmer (Swimming World Publications, P.O. Box 45497, Los Angeles, CA 90045). This is a wonderful magazine for junior level, high school, and college swimmers.

Organizations

American Swimming Coaches Association (ASCA). This organization seeks to ensure standard levels of coaching throughout the United States. For further information, write to 1 Hall of Fame Dr., Ft. Lauderdale, FL 33316, or call (305) 462-6267.

College Swimming Coaches Association of America. Promotes college swimming throughout the country. Write to 111 Cooke Hall, University of Minnesota, Minneapolis, MN 55455.

International Amateur Swimming Federation (Fédération Internationale de Natation Amateur, or FINA). The international governing body for amateur competitive swimming. Offers a handbook of international rules through United States Swimming (see below). Write to 1750 East Boulder St., Colorado Springs, CO 80909, or call (719) 578-4578.

International Swimming Hall of Fame. A fascinating collection of swimming memorabilia and information on swimming's greatest competitors. Write to 1 Hall of Fame Dr., Fort Lauderdale, FL 33316, or call (305) 462-6536 for information about hours, publications, souvenirs, and services offered.

National Association of Intercollegiate Athletics (NAIA). The governing body for all member institutions' competitive athletic programs. Write to 1221 Baltimore, Kansas City, MO 64105, or call (816) 842-5050.

National Collegiate Athletic Association (NCAA). The governing body for all member institutions' competitive athletic programs. Write to 6201 College Blvd., Overland Park, KS 66211-2422, or call (913) 339-1906.

National Interscholastic Swimming Coaches Association (NISCA). Promotes high-school swimming throughout the U.S. Write to Glenn Kaye, President, South Broward H. S., 23181-B Fountain View, Boca Raton, FL 33433, or call (407) 750-1255.

National Jewish Welfare Board. Provides information about swim meets at local YM-YWHAs. Write to 15 East 26th St., New York, NY 10010, or call (212) 532-4949.

National Junior College Athletic Association (NJCAA). The governing body for most junior-college athletics in the U.S. Write to P.O. Box 7305, Colorado Springs, CO 80933, or call (719) 590-9788.

National Young Men's Christian Association (YMCA). Provides information about local YMCA Masters swim programs, plus addresses of YM-YWCAs nationwide. Write to 291 Broadway, New York, NY 10007, or call (212) 374-2150.

National Young Women's Christian Association (YWCA). Write to 600 Lexington Ave., New York, NY 10022, or call (212) 753-4700.

United States Masters Swimming. The official organization for Masters swimming in the U.S. If you're over 19, you can become a member and partake of the organization's publications, clinics, and other resources. Write to 2 Peter Ave., Rutland, MA 01543, or call Dorothy Donnelly at (508) 886-6631.

United States Swimming. The national governing body for amateur swimming in the United States and the source for the official rules for Senior, Age Group/Jr. Olympic, and Long Distance amateur competitive swimming programs. Write to 1750 East Boulder St., Colorado Springs, CO 80909, or call (719) 578-4578.